RECRUITMENT
TO SKILLED TRADES

INTERNATIONAL LIBRARY OF SOCIOLOGY AND SOCIAL RECONSTRUCTION

Founded by Karl Mannheim
Editor: W. J. H. Sprott

Catalogue of the books available in the INTERNATIONAL LIBRARY OF SOCIOLOGY AND SOCIAL RECONSTRUCTION and new books in preparation for the Library will be found at the end of this volume

RECRUITMENT
TO SKILLED
TRADES

by Gertrude Williams

LONDON
ROUTLEDGE & KEGAN PAUL
NEW YORK: HUMANITIES PRESS

First published in 1957
by Routledge & Kegan Paul Ltd
Broadway House
68–74 Carter Lane
London EC4
© *by Gertrude Williams*
Printed in Great Britain
by Butler & Tanner Ltd
Frome and London

CONTENTS

v

PREFACE

THE research on which this book is based was carried out with the aid of a grant made available under the Conditional Aid Scheme for the use of Counterpart Funds derived from United States Economic Aid; and I am glad to have this opportunity to express my gratitude for this assistance.

My thanks are due also to a very large number of people who answered written enquiries or who gave valuable time out of busy working days to personal interviews. They are too numerous for it to be possible to name each individually; but this enquiry could not have been completed without the co-operation of personnel managers and apprentice masters all over the country, principals and staffs of technical colleges, secretaries of trade unions and employers' associations and officials of government departments who have given me generously of their time and knowledge. My thanks are no less warm for being offered collectively.

I should like also to express my appreciation of the help given me throughout the three years taken by the enquiry by my research assistant, Mr. John Hopson, and my secretary Mrs. Doreen Edgar, without whose unflagging co-operation, the task would have been much more burdensome than it was.

GERTRUDE WILLIAMS

Bedford College,
July 1957

I

THE HISTORICAL BACKGROUND

UNTIL the beginning of the nineteenth century the usual
method of entry to trade and industry in general was through
apprenticeship. The master undertook to teach the boy
placed under his care everything necessary to enable him to
become, first a journeyman, and later a master of the business, and the boy undertook to serve his master faithfully
during the term of years laid down, at a wage well below the
customary rate for an adult in that occupation. It was usual
for the apprentice to lodge with his master and to learn from
him not only the details of the craft or business but also the
general knowledge of life and manners considered suitable to
his degree.

This contractual relationship was formally established by
the Statute of Artificers passed in 1562, which became the
foundation of a national system of apprenticeship. By this
Act a period of seven years' servitude was imposed on all
those who wished to set up in any trade or craft, and as far as
the Law was concerned a person who had not undergone this
period of training was not entitled to set up as a master for
himself. The Act was not repealed until 1814 but long before
that date its provisions had ceased to be widely effective. In
many trades no questions were asked of a journeyman about
the length of time he had served, and masters took on as
many young people as they wished without any form of
either written or verbal agreement with regard to their training. Even more important than the latitude in observance of
the clauses of the Statute was the fact that it was held not to

apply to 'new' trades, so that all the developments in industry and commerce of the seventeenth and eighteenth centuries were outside its scope. So great in fact were the changes that had taken place by the beginning of the nineteenth century that it is believed that in all probability 99% of the journey-men then working would have been doing so illegally if the Statute had been enforced.

But although conditions had changed, the use of the term 'apprentice' still remained for young workers. The Poor Law authorities, who in the early years of the last century farmed out pauper children to the cotton mills, spoke of them as apprentices although there was no longer any obligation on the employer to teach them anything other than the simple mechanical processes for which he was anxious to procure them. They were apprentices only in the sense that they were bound to the employer with whom they had been placed throughout the period of their minority, but in actual fact they were simply cheap child labour. As mechanical pro-cesses were introduced into one industry after another this use of child labour became more and more common, though the children were sons and daughters of 'free' parents rather than the protegés of the Poor Law Officers, and apprentice-ship as a period of supervised training for a skilled job came gradually to be confined to a comparatively small number of occupations—those in which, despite the introduction of machinery, there was still need for both manipulative skill and understanding of the processes. For this comparatively small number of trades there had grown up two distinct, though related, methods of entry. In some, apprenticeship retained unchanged the features that had characterized it for centuries; boys were bound by written indentures for a term of years, and the reciprocal obligations of master and youth were clearly stated. Although the Statute of Artificers was repealed and there was therefore no legal regulation of this period of training, the trade unions which grew up in the skilled crafts in the mid-nineteenth century made careful arrangements about the period of training and the field of recruitment from which apprentices might be chosen. Where no such traditional form of apprenticeship remained there

2

were crafts in which the journeymen had been allowed to introduce and train their own sons. In this case there was no indenture, no fixed term of training, no conditions of employment laid down and no regulation covering the numbers to be admitted. A journeyman could, if he wished, introduce and train all his sons at once, or allow one to follow another as he reached the age for employment. In some occupations workers who were childless were entitled to introduce the sons of fellow-workers, but in others the privilege was retained strictly for members of one's own family. In still other trades there was a combination of both methods. An apprentice was indentured to the employer but the employer undertook to restrict the choice to sons of those already working in the trade.

The general purpose of the regulations which were enforced either by custom or trade union agreement was to control entry to the trade, so as to protect skilled workers from competition for jobs from outsiders; but there were industries, and particularly those which were expanding greatly during the second half of the last century, in which the unions' sphere of organization was not sufficiently comprehensive to make the restrictions fully effective. In the printing industry, for example, which required a certain standard of education as well as manual dexterity, a seven-year apprenticeship had been universal in the eighteenth century, and although much machinery was later introduced the industry still demanded skill of a high order. But the spread of industry and commerce into new areas led to the demand for a great deal of printing work in areas in which there were no long-established printing firms, most of which, naturally enough, had congregated in the large towns. There sprang up therefore a very large number of firms, mainly small in size, but some of quite considerable extent, to provide for the needs of the new industrial areas, and the printing trade unions did not manage to keep pace in their organization with this diffusion of the industry over the country. In most of the small firms that sprang up in the new localities the regulations that the printing unions had struggled to maintain were rarely observed. There was no regulation of entry, no restriction of the number of young employees, and no specific training. Boys picked up the craft as well as they could and when they grew older offered themselves to other firms first as 'improvers' and then as qualified craftsmen, and in this way many of them gradually drifted into the big centres, where they provided the fringe of adult workers who were taken on by expanding firms without any awkward questions being asked as to where they had served their apprenticeship. The unions were faced with a difficult dilemma. If they refused to admit these workers as full members of the union they could act as blacklegs and undermine the wage rates fixed by collective agreement, and if they did admit them they virtually threw overboard their regulations covering the period of training and the ratio of apprentices to journeymen. In fact, they found it less dangerous to admit them as full members, and thus it was only in the highest class work where skill of an exceptional order was required that the regulations applied in all their force.

Much the same situation was found in the engineering industry and for the same reasons. The rules of the Amalgamated Society of Engineers in 1864 declared that

'if constrained to make restrictions against the admission into our trade of those who have not earned the right by probationary servitude we do so knowing that such engagements are productive of evil and when persevered in unchecked result in reducing the condition of the artisan to that of the unskilled labourer and confer no permanent advantage on those admitted. It is our duty then to exercise the same care and watchfulness over that in which we have a vested interest as the physician does who holds a diploma or the author who is protected by a copyright'.

Yet the mechanization and specialization of the various branches of engineering were making it at once more difficult for a boy to get a general training and less necessary in view of much of the work he was called upon to do, and in practice the A.S.E. found it expedient to admit to membership anybody who could show he had worked for five years in an engineering establishment, whether he had been apprenticed or not, and who at the time of his application for

4

admission was receiving the standard rate of wages for his particular section of the industry.

This difficulty in excluding 'illegal men' from the trade unions resulted in the breakdown of apprenticeship regulations in one industry after another until the regular period of servitude was confined only to the highest quality of workmanship in the biggest centres of work where the union officials could keep a watchful eye on what was being done.

From the time of the repeal of the Statute of Artificers until recently the main concern of those with some knowledge of juvenile labour has been directed more towards protecting young people from the ignorance and cupidity of parents and employers than towards provision for the selection and training of those who were to become skilled workers. A long series of Factory Acts beginning in 1801, and two Education Acts beginning in 1870, finally had the effect of completely excluding children from factory employment, and with each raising of the legal school-leaving age the period of 'childhood' has been extended. But for those young people whom the Law considered old enough to be in employment very little was done in the way of protecting them from exploitation or of ensuring that they received any training which would fit them for regular or more skilled employment in the future. In fact, everything conspired to push young workers into jobs which had little constructive value as training grounds for the future, either as workers or as citizens. By the turn of the century the trade unions covered only about a million and a quarter workers, and in most occupations wages were so low that men had a hard task to make both ends meet, for family responsibilities were generally heavy. Although the birth-rate began to fall in the 'eighties and 'nineties, a typical wage-earning family still consisted of five or six children, and the burden on the father while they were all still of school age was such as to drag him very close to the poverty line. Social insurance schemes had not yet begun and earnings had to be stretched to cover frequent periods of unemployment and sickness. It was small wonder then that parents were anxious to get their children into some

5

wage-earning employment at the earliest possible moment. To allow even one child to take a period of industrial training involved great sacrifices on the part of the parents, for the wages received by apprentices were extremely low. To train more than one involved a burden that could not be contemplated. Boys and girls thus snatched at any job that became available at the moment they left school, irrespective of whether it would lead to any employment in the future.

At the same time, changes in techniques and in industrial structure were opening the door to people with no industrial training. The increased use of machinery and the rapid development of large-scale production led to the breakdown of skilled jobs into semi-skilled processes which could be learned in a few days or at most a few weeks. Many of these processes were well within the scope of school-leavers and the low wages that children were ready to accept in order to get a foot inside the industrial door gave them an advantage over the older workers. Most of these juvenile employees were dismissed after a couple of years' time when they began to demand higher wages and their places were taken by the more recent recruits to the field of employment. Thus the older adolescent found himself with no job, no skill, no training and no experience of any value to fit him for adult work. The Royal Commission on the Poor Law of 1909 was much concerned with the flow of unskilled adults fit for nothing other than the lowest types of casual labour which came from these blind alley types of employment, and urged the importance of some machinery to guide young people into work that would lead to more regular employment.

Even before the Report of the Royal Commission those with first-hand knowledge of the problems of young workers had been struck by the same idea, and certain voluntary societies, notably the Jewish Board of Guardians which cared for the Jewish poor in the East End of London and other areas in which Jewish labourers mainly congregated, attempted to revive the idea of apprenticeship as a safeguard for young workers. The first 'Apprenticeship and Skilled Employment Committee' was established in 1897 and by 1905 there were enough such committees in London, Liverpool, and a few other cities for the local societies to join together to form the Apprenticeship and Skilled Employment Association with a central office in London. The purpose of these committees was to find suitable openings for boys and girls who applied to them for help and who seemed capable of learning a trade and willing to do so. They made terms with the employers with the aim of securing fair conditions to both learner and master and held a watching brief throughout the period of training. The committees recognized that apprenticeship was suitable to only a minority of trades and they did not attempt to reintroduce it where technical developments had rendered it unnecessary. They could deal therefore with only a tiny proportion of young workers, but nevertheless their work was of value. By collecting information they threw much-needed light on the conditions of employment of young people, and called attention to the need for a more serious concern with the entry into employment of adolescent labour.

Young people however were not in any exceptional position in being left to fend for themselves in their search for employment. One of the surprising things about our industrial development is the slowness with which it was realized that there is a need for the organization of a labour market. It was taken for granted that workers would always know, or could easily find out, where jobs were vacant, and a large amount of unnecessary unemployment or unsuitable employment took place solely because of the lack of any clearing house of information from which employers might learn of available workers and workers find out where they could apply for jobs. Some few trade unions maintained registers of vacancies for their own trades and some highly skilled trades normally used the advertisement columns of the daily newspapers but, for the most part, those seeking work had to rely on the advice they picked up from friends and acquaintances or were forced to tramp wearily from place to place in hope of seeing a factory notice saying 'Hands Wanted'. It was not until 1909 that, with the passing of the Labour Exchange Act, there began to be established that national network of information offices which we now call employment exchanges and which has so radically changed the whole labour market.

From the outset it was recognized that the needs of young people were different from those of the adult worker. The grown man has already some industrial experience and has come to identify himself and to be identified by employers with certain types of work. What he needs is first to know where such work is available to him and second what other closely allied jobs might be worth trying if there is no vacancy of the exact type to which he is accustomed. The main function of the employment exchange for him is to marry suitable vacancies to suitable applicants. But for the young worker something more far-reaching is required. He has potentialities rather than achievements. There may be several different occupations into which he might be fitted, and it will be of immense importance to his future industrial career for him to go into the field that fits his abilities and at the same time is likely to offer continuous employment. At the age of 14 or 15 he could do equally well in any one of half a dozen jobs; at 19 or 20 his abilities and experience have become canalized and it is no longer so easy for him to move from one occupation to another. For the young worker then guidance in the choice of an occupation is as important as, if not more important than, finding an available vacancy.

The early recognition of the importance of vocational guidance led to some debate as to the best source from which such help should come. The officials of the newly set up labour exchanges might be able to acquire much information about possible openings in the industries located in their area, but there was no reason to suppose that they had any special capacity for assessing the abilities of the young people who were in need of jobs. There were many people who felt that the first few years of industrial employment should be treated as a continuation of the educational process rather than as part of adult industrial life. For both these reasons the education authority might, it was thought, prove a more suitable body to look after the employment problems of adolescent workers. But to compel them to do so might mean falling between two stools. The education authorities would not have the industrial knowledge that it was the function of the labour exchanges to acquire, and unless their members were particularly concerned with, and sympathetic to these problems there would be nobody who would make it his province to organize and administer a constructive scheme. For these reasons it was decided to give education authorities the opportunity to engage in this work without compelling them to do so. Those which wished to make themselves responsible for guiding the young were given legal permission to do so and in those localities the labour exchanges withdrew from the care of the adolescent worker; but in areas in which the local education authority did not choose to exercise the right, the function devolved upon the labour exchanges. There thus began a dual system which has remained to the present day, although (as will be shown later) it has recently undergone fundamental reorganization.

In general, both authorities operated in much the same way and, it must be confessed, with much the same lack of success. Talks were given to school-leavers about the occupations in the locality, conferences were held with the teachers and the parents of those in their final school term, and advice, most of it, unhappily, backed by little real knowledge, was hopefully given. As a matter of fact, however, most of the placings of young people were not made through the offices—either those of the local education authority or of the employment exchanges—but young workers got themselves in and out of jobs much in the same ways as they had before the statutory machinery was set up. Some depended on fathers and older brothers to put in a word for them, some answered advertisements, some were helped by school-teachers or social workers and a great many relied on themselves. Only about a third of first jobs were got through official channels, and after the first job it was much less usual for adolescent workers voluntarily to return for further advice or help. As an overall figure therefore the number of placings done by statutory agencies was not more than about 20% for young workers below the age of 18.

Even during the twenty years between the two wars when mass unemployment was a chronic feature of the British economy, it was in general not difficult for school-leavers to find their first jobs. The big expansion of mass production, particularly in the consumption trades, opened up many avenues of employment for untrained workers and the low wages commonly paid to juveniles gave them an advantage over their elders. It is significant that Arnold Freeman, writing in 1914 on Boy Labour, mentions 'semi-skilled' as a new term, and even the New Survey of London Life and Labour[1] published in 1931 thought it necessary to draw attention to the rise of an intermediate class of semi-skilled workers unknown in the past, who obtained their training by moving up a 'ladder of progressively complex processes'. For such process workers steadiness and care, rather than skill in the craftsman's sense of the word, were required, and young workers could easily learn to do most of these jobs. By the middle of the first World War the proportion of boys to men had almost doubled in the building industry and had increased by 50% in engineering.

But whilst mechanization increased the proportion of jobs that can be done with little formal teaching or experience it also brought into being the demand for skill of the highest order to make the tools and to set and maintain the complex machines operated by the semi-skilled. For this highly skilled nucleus of workers apprenticeship, supplemented by instruction in the technical schools, was still essential. There were other kinds of work which came somewhere between these two extremes requiring more than careful repetition of a single process but not the comprehensive knowledge of those competent to deal with processes and intricate tools. For this group a period of learnership was customary; and these in their turn shaded off into occupations in which a worker without any definite instruction might be upgraded from simpler to more complex processes as he showed himself capable of undertaking more difficult tasks.

The first war did much to expand the proportion of repetition and process work to skilled craft work; for with the shortage of highly qualified men and the absolute need to increase production, particularly in the engineering indus-

[1] Vol. II, p. 10.

tries, much inventive genius was concentrated on the task of breaking down skilled jobs into their constituent processes on which semi-skilled men and women might be employed. The war thus did much to accelerate the development which was already strongly under way, and opened the door in industries which had traditionally been considered highly skilled to workers with no particular qualifications. By the 'twenties therefore three separate ways of training recruits for skilled occupations were in force:

(1) Apprenticeship: that is a contractual relationship in the traditional sense in which the employer bound himself to teach a boy—or cause him to be taught—the trade or business, and in which the worker undertook to serve for a stated period of time at wages which were below the standard rate for the job when it was done by a skilled adult. Such a contract did not necessarily take the form of an indenture nor was it always a written agreement of a less formal nature. A verbal undertaking in which both sides recognized the customary terms was sufficient, and in practice, this 'gentleman's agreement' was by far the most usual type of contract. The essential part of it was the obligation on the part of the employer to see that the apprentice was taught all that a skilled craftsman should know (though sometimes this was customarily limited by acceptance of the fact that the employer could teach only that part of the craft that was carried on in his business, and that the apprentice might equally have a limited capacity to learn).

In the days when apprenticeship was the only legal means of entry to a trade it had been usual for fathers to buy their sons in by paying a premium for an indenture and though this had long fallen into general disuse there was still a certain proportion of such premiums paid. The practice varied from trade to trade and region to region. Over 16% of shipbuilding apprentices in the mid-twenties had had premiums paid on their behalf whilst in engineering there were only 5–7%, and in printing and building between 2 and 3%. Even so, the premiums were usually so small as to be almost 'token'— rarely more than £10, and sometimes as little as £1.

Apprenticeship was confined to relatively few occupations.

It was found mainly in the engineering and allied industries, in shipbuilding, building, wood-working, printing and a few others.

(2) Learnership: a form of training of comparatively recent origin. The learner was not an apprentice but was taken on for a specific period of years, usually less than that required for apprenticeship, and was given definite facilities to learn a branch of the trade or a particular process. The agreement was extremely vague but the most important characteristic was that there was no specific obligation on the employer to teach but merely to allow the boy facilities for learning by watching others with whom he was in contact. This form of training was usual in textiles, boot and shoe and paper-making and in the group of industries covered by Trade Board regulations.

(3) Upgrading: this was the practice of promoting labourers or unskilled workers to semi-skilled or even higher jobs as a result of learning by association with more skilled persons. A quick and observant man who had acted for some time as a 'mate' to a skilled worker might, if there were a shortage of suitable workers, be allowed to try his hand during a sudden rush of work. If this happened fairly frequently the less complex or less intricate parts of the craftsman's job might come to be left to him as a regular thing. During the latter years of the first World War this practice became more general, for the supply of fully qualified craftsmen was so severely restricted. As many skilled men had joined the Forces there were not enough skilled men to train apprentices and even those who remained were less willing to take time off to instruct young workers when piece rates began to be introduced. At the same time the higher wages that boys could get on unskilled or semi-skilled work, coupled with the knowledge that in any case their industrial training would be interrupted by the call-up at 18, lessened the readiness both of boys and their parents to undertake a long period of apprenticeship.

An enquiry into training for skilled trades made by the Ministry of Labour in the mid-twenties shows that in those occupations in which apprenticeship was supposed to be the rule rather less than a quarter of all employers had in fact any apprentices to train. The proportion showed a wide variation from one trade to another, from shipbuilding at one extreme in which 88·5% had apprentices, to the brick and tile industry at the other with less than 8%. Printing with 62%, engineering and iron and steel with 53% and building with 36%, come in the middle.

As a general thing apprentices were concentrated in the small rather than the larger firms. In the printing industry, for example, the proportion of apprentices to all male workers was 1 : 35 in firms employing 500 or more and 1 : 2·7 in those with less than five employees. In building the variation ran from 1 : 23 to 1 : 2·4 and in engineering from 1 : 13·6 to 1 : 2·3 over the same range of size. In printing this was not surprising for the trade unions maintained a strict limit on the number of apprentices that a firm might take, irrespective of its size; and in other industries it was perhaps partly to be accounted for by the much larger clerical and ancillary staff in the larger firms. But a good deal of the variation derived from the fact that the larger firms usually had more highly specialized mass-production methods whilst the smaller were more varied and so both required workers with more skilled qualifications, and had a greater diversity of jobs on which to train them. To a certain extent also parents preferred to place their boys with smaller firms because they believed that they would get more individual attention in this way, but there is no doubt that much of the difference was due to the unwillingness of larger firms to be bothered with apprentices when experience showed them that they could generally rely on getting their skilled workers when they wanted them ready trained from the smaller competitor.

The ratio of apprentices to the total of male adult employees is however a somewhat unreal figure. The increase in the scale of the production unit inevitably alters the allocation of manpower between direct productive processes on the one hand and distribution, transport and clerical activities on the other. What is really significant is the extent to which provision is made for the recruitment and training of skilled workers to replace those currently at work; but unfortunately there were no figures available at the time of the enquiry to show the numbers of skilled workers from which such a calculation might have been made. Only in the case of the printing and building industries was there any direct evidence and for the others it was necessary to make an estimate based mainly on comparison with the figures of the Census of 1921. As these estimates however are remarkably in line with the known ratios in building and printing it is likely that they are not very far from the truth.

According to these figures, then, the ratio of apprentices to skilled workers varied from 1 : 4½ to 1 : 6. Some of the crafts included in shipbuilding showed the highest ratio of 1 : 2½ adult skilled men, and motor repairs showed least with fewer than 1 : 6 adults but in most crafts and most areas 1 : 4 or 5 was fairly common.

Despite the low wages paid to apprentices there seems to have been little difficulty in attracting boys. True, many employers complained that they had not got the type of boy they liked and that they used to have; but it is impossible to determine to what extent this criticism was part of the general 'young people are not what they were when I was a boy' and how far it was based on some real change in the type of young people who wished to qualify. Certainly boys who became apprentices had to have an eye to the future, for even though wages in ordinary jobs were not very generous the pay received by trainees meant a considerable sacrifice during the training years. Yet the competition of these alternative occupations did have some influence, for the actual pay earned by apprentices varied, even in the same craft, from area to area according to the openings available in other industries. In engineering, for example, the pay of apprentices varied between 8s. and 13s. in the first year and from 20s. to 32s. in the last; in building from 8s. to 15s. in the first year and 20s. to 47s. 8d. in the last; in printing from 10s. to 15s. in the first and 25s. to 45s. in the last; but in shipbuilding, usually carried on in areas where few other industries competed, the ratios were from 8s. to 12s. 6d. in the first year and 17s. to 24s. 6d. in the last. These rates were always time rates and in the last year of the apprenticeship represented about 40% to 50% of the journeyman's rate in the same craft. Even after the end of the formal apprenticeship the young man did not rise at once to the standard rate of pay. There was usually a short period to be spent as an 'improver' at 75% of the journeyman's rate before the worker was considered fully qualified. In non-apprenticed occupations on the other hand the pay of a 15-year-old boy (the age at which apprenticeship generally began) ranged from 9s. to 28s. 4d. and for a boy of 19 from 22s. 3d. to 56s. 9d. In these circumstances it is surprising how rare it was for an apprenticeship to be given up; in printing the wastage rate was as low as 1·3% and in building 2·2% and even in shipbuilding where the rate was highest it was not more than 10%. Having once embarked on it the vast majority of apprentices remained on, and with the same employer, until qualified. Nor was this due to extreme care in selection. In many firms indeed, provided the boy looked reasonably fit physically and was not obviously mentally defective, this was all that was required. If there were more applicants than vacancies the preference was almost invariably given to the sons of employees or to those who came with some personal recommendation or in some few cases, mainly engineering firms, boys from secondary or technical schools were welcome.

As the school-leaving age gradually went up, in the early years of the century, so too did the age of entry into apprenticeship until by the mid-twenties 15½ to 16 was by far the most usual, and it seems as if for this reason and no other the period of apprenticeship had tended to fall slightly. For the period of training was fixed not by the amount to be learnt (for it would be a remarkable coincidence if all crafts, however much they varied in nature, took exactly the same amount of time to master), but by trade union regulation. For some reason the age of 21 has always played a significant part in union wage agreements and it was the insistence on the absolute necessity of paying a man of 21 the full adult rate for the job that both fixed the age of entry and the period of training. The seven-year training that had been usual was itself arbitrary and had been fixed partly by long-standing custom and partly by the need to ensure that the apprentice-ship ended at the age of legal majority when a boy might have the power to repudiate a contract made in his name if he wished to do so. As the school-leaving age was raised the period was reduced to five or six years so as to ensure that it still finished at 21, and unions were adamant that the age of entry should not be more than 16 in order to allow for a minimum of five years' apprenticeship before the age of 21 was reached.

It was the length of apprenticeship rather than the type of training given to which the unions attached most importance. Some few firms had organized apprenticeship schemes with carefully systematized plans of training and had even in some cases established Works Schools; but the vast majority of apprentices learned their trade by being put under the charge of a skilled worker whose work they watched and to whom they acted as 'mate'. In almost all cases the first few months or even the first year was largely wasted. The boy acted as messenger or 'tea-boy' and what he learnt depended primarily on his own enthusiasm and keenness of observa-tion. Not all of this was completely useless for it was necessary for the young worker to learn the layout of the factory and to become familiar with the names of the tools, materials and processes, but this could have been done in a very much shorter time if any care had been directed to introducing the boy to the job and giving him a few weeks of tuition. Much of the time was wasted because of the unwillingness of the worker under whom the apprentice was theoretically training to lay off his own work in order to instruct a beginner. In some firms an extra payment was made to the adult to whom the apprentice was attached so as to compensate him for the interruption in his own work, but even so the benefit to the trainee depended partly on the variety of jobs that the skilled worker had to do and very much on his ability to impart his knowledge to somebody else. Most craftsmen are more skilled with their hands than with their tongues and it is only rarely that a man who is master of his trade has the imaginative insight to understand the difficulties and pro-blems of somebody going newly to it; so that even where the adult worker took his job of instruction seriously it was not always very well done. The whole system was haphazard and casual and it was nobody's responsibility to ensure that the boy had the opportunity to learn the various branches of his trade nor that, even if he had the opportunity, he had, in fact, managed to reach a certain standard of competence. So long as he had put in the required number of years he was entitled to call himself a skilled worker and receive the appropriate rate of pay. Those who did not, in fact, receive a good all-round training or who had not the ability to profit from it probably found it more difficult later on to get and to hold down a job; but this depended mainly on the demand for workers in their locality when they became adult.

The proportion of boys undergoing apprenticeship was however extremely small—only $13\frac{1}{2}\%$ of those under 21 in all industries. If we add to this number all those getting some form of training in manual work the proportion is still not very large—only 1 in 5 of youths under 21. The other 80% received no training at all but were employed in unskilled or semi-skilled operations. Of the 20% who were either apprentices or learners four-fifths were to be found in one small group of industries—shipbuilding, engineering and other metal industries, building, printing, wood-working and retail trade. But the vast majority of boys left school at 14 and took up whatever job happened to be available in the neighbourhood.

There was a great deal of disquiet about this situation amongst those whose work brought them into intimate contact with adolescence. But the tragedy of the period between the two wars was that the immense shadow of chronic mass-unemployment hung so black and menacing over the industrial scene as to blot out almost everything else. With so much adult unemployment in the basic industries and particularly in those such as shipbuilding, building and certain branches of engineering, in which as has been stated the largest amount of skilled work was to be found, little concern was felt about the flow of skilled workers for the future. It was not until the second World War swept all adult labour into the Forces or into essential industry that the shortage of qualified men able to undertake jobs which required detailed knowledge and experience in handling precision tools began to force itself upon the attention. Skilled men were at a premium and in many works the expansion of the repetition processes was held up because of the impossibility of getting hold of the nucleus of key workmen able to set and supervise the machines. The supply of men of such a type cannot however be rapidly increased, for it requires years of training, and whilst a certain amount could be done during the emergency to train people rapidly in certain branches of the work or to break down complicated jobs into their component processes, questions began to be asked about the future. Already early in the war it was realized that the end of hostilities would usher in a period of tremendous effort if industries were to recapture their export markets, and that this would be impossible without an adequate supply of trained workers. Unless the matter were taken in hand at once these workers would not be forthcoming when they were most needed.

There were two other factors that tended also to direct attention towards this neglected problem. The first was the decline in the number of young people available for employment. For some time before the war demographers had been trying to stimulate some comprehension of the importance of the falling birth-rate which has characterized the present century, but without any significant success. At the outbreak of war there were nearly 100,000 young workers without jobs and even this figure showed a great improvement on the situation of a few years earlier. There were so many young people who had had practically no work since they left school that a great many people were more inclined to think that new recruits to employment were far in excess of what was needed by industry rather than likely to be scarce, and at this time there was even much talk in some quarters of the urgency of persuading more young people to emigrate to other parts of the Commonwealth where they might find better opportunities than seemed available at home.

The general change in the manpower situation brought about by the war compelled people to take a more realistic view of the state of affairs. At the end of the first World War the fall in the birth-rate had been temporarily halted and for four years the rate was considerably higher than it had been for some time. Fourteen years later this resulted in an adolescent bulge which reached its peak in 1937 when the group between 14 and 18 consisted of $3\frac{1}{4}$ million boys and girls. Not all of these were available for employment. A small percentage remained at school and a much smaller proportion were either physically unfit for work or did not need to earn. But the vast majority of this group constituted the juvenile labour force. From that year however the total fell rapidly, for during the 'thirties the birth-rate had shown its most rapid decrease until it reached its lowest point in the late 'thirties, with a rate of 14·7, so that in the early 'forties the number in the 14–18 age group was smaller by half a million than it had been in 1937. Nothing, it was realized, could prevent it from falling further still, for each group reaching the school-leaving age and entering into employment was smaller than the one which had preceded it.

Educational policy reduced the number of adolescent workers still further, for the rise in the school-leaving age, which had been a matter of bitter controversy during the 'thirties, was now accepted by all parties as a change to be introduced at the earliest possible moment. In fact it was included in the Education Act of 1944 and this meant that in future there would be only a three-year group in the juvenile workers instead of a four-year one as heretofore.

The second factor which played its part in bringing the problem of the young worker into the forefront of discussion was a development in the sense of social responsibility which was also in part a consequence of the war. There was a strong feeling that workers had had a raw deal during the miseries of the 'thirties and that much more needed to be done both to prevent the wastage of ability and to ensure that the ordinary average person without any unusual capacity might have the opportunity to develop himself to the fullest extent of which he was capable. The registration of boys and girls which began in 1941 brought to light so much waste in the lives of young people as a result of overwork, lack of training and of supervision, and on account of the scarcity of opportunities for development, that much shame was felt that the community had for so long ignored the most precious of its natural resources, the younger generation. And the newly awakened understanding that these natural resources were becoming scarcer with each successive year spurred people on to a consideration of a more constructive policy.

Two consequences were the direct result of this change in attitude, both of which were of importance in their effects on the youth labour market. The first was an organized effort to improve the methods by which industries recruit and train their young workers; the second a comprehensive survey of the machinery for guiding and placing young workers in search of jobs.

In 1942 the Ministry of Labour initiated discussions with the Joint Consultative Committee representing the British Employers' Confederation and the Trades Union Congress with regard to the post-war situation. Discussions with representative industries later took place and the Joint Consultative Committee presented a Report to the Minister on the Recruitment and Training of Juveniles for Industry, which made suggestions for the recruitment and training of young persons after the war. The developments which resulted from these recommendations are the subject of the next chapter.

Three years after the publication of this report, early in 1945, the Minister of Labour set up a Committee under the Chairmanship of Sir Godfrey Ince, Permanent Secretary to the Ministry, to investigate the working of the statutory machinery for advising young people. The Committee consisted of representatives of the Trades Union Congress, the British Employers' Confederation, the local authorities, and the three Government departments concerned—the Ministry of Labour, the Ministry of Education and the Scottish Department of Education. It was widely felt that the dual system whereby responsibility was divided between the Ministry of Labour and the local education authorities had not been successful and that a more closely integrated system was needed. But whilst the members of the committee shared this general opinion, they were equally divided on the important question whether the educational or the labour authority was the more suitable department to have the sole responsibility. Should the first few years of industrial life be considered primarily as an extension of the educational process in a different sphere or primarily as an introduction to the world of adult employment? In the first case the Ministry of Education is obviously the right body to look after the young worker, in the second place the Ministry of Labour should be responsible. There was much to be said for each view. The young worker, whether he is undergoing a form of apprenticeship or not, is certainly in need of guidance and care, and the local education authorities have very much more knowledge of the capacities and psychological make-up of young people than have the employment exchanges. Very close contact with the schools gives them a fund of material on which to draw in assessing the aptitudes and intellectual abilities of young people. Moreover, since the war, local education authorities have had placed upon them the responsibility for ensuring that facilities for constructive leisure and development should be available for adolescents in their locality, and the Education Act of 1944 included provision for County Colleges, attendance at which for eight hours a week would become obligatory on all young workers. In this case it seemed sensible that the authority that was looking after the young worker for one part of his working life and had the responsibility for caring for him during his leisure, should also be responsible for guiding him into employment and supervising him during working hours. Experience had shown that the local education authorities had an additional advantage for, as each authority is within wide limits autonomous in its own area, there is a possibility of experiment that cannot be introduced so easily into a national service. Several of the local education authorities which had taken their function of supervising young workers very seriously had introduced many valuable innovations, such as psychological and intelligence tests, to enable them to get a more accurate assessment of the abilities of the young people to whom they were giving advice.

On the other hand there were equally strong arguments in favour of leaving the job to the Ministry of Labour, for whilst a young worker is undoubtedly learning he is also earning and is in fact much more an employed person than he is a pupil. To make a sharp division between the first three years of his industrial life and the remaining forty-seven seemed to have little real justification. This view was strengthened when it was remembered that the Ministry of Labour is responsible for the general supervision of working conditions through the Factory Acts, and that its officials have an immense fund of detailed knowledge of industrial organization and industrial developments as a necessary part of their work in dealing with adult employees. Two other advantages were seen to be enjoyed by the Ministry of Labour. As a national body it cannot, it is true, experiment with the same ease as can a local authority in its more restricted field, but it can on the other hand maintain a minimum standard of performance in a way that is not open to a system which is based on purely local administration; and in the past the work of the juvenile departments of the local offices, while they fell far below the standard of the most adventurous and most responsible local education authorities, were far above the achievements of the large number which treated their vocational guidance functions rather cavalierly. Moreover, a national service has the advantage of transcending local boundaries which are often, particularly in urban areas, extremely artificial. A local education authority has power only within its own area and this narrows the variety of openings in which it can place the young recruit to industry. The Ministry of Labour is not restricted in this sense either in knowledge or power. It can put its knowledge of industrial opportunities in other areas at the service of young people in one particular locality and through its clearing system it can make the administrative arrangements necessary for placing them in touch with suitable vacancies in other areas.

With the arguments in favour of the two departments so narrowly balanced, it was impossible for the Committee to make up its mind to put the scheme in the care solely of either one or the other, and the plan it finally recommended was designed to combine the best features of both authorities whilst overcoming the disadvantages that had emanated from the dual control of the past. Their recommendations were the basis of the system introduced by the Education and Training Act of 1948. By this Act the local education authorities retained the power to undertake this service provided they prepared approved schemes within a given time limit, but the whole system whether organized by a local education authority or the Ministry of Labour was placed under the central authority of a new body designed for the purpose—the Central Youth Employment Executive. In this way it was hoped to get both local concern with its freedom to experiment, together with national integration and maintenance of uniform standards of administrative competence. An obligation was laid upon the schools to co-operate in areas where the Ministry of Labour was the responsible authority so that the Youth Employment Officers might have full knowledge of the activities and records of school-leavers. As much reliance is placed on all youth work on the value of contact with non-official bodies and people, the administrative machinery made provisions for advisory bodies on a national and local basis. In this way it was hoped to ensure a constant assessment of the value of the services both as a national system and at the local level.

Apart from this new administrative set-up the Act introduced an innovation that might prove of great value. Most young people start work at 15 when their earnings are inadequate to maintain them away from home and when, quite apart from financial considerations, they are too young to live without parental care. It is not merely control and supervision that may be needed but, much more important, affection and interest. The change from school life to employment is drastic, in any case, and most young people depend greatly on parents and brothers and sisters for the sense of security which helps them to make the adjustment. This inevitably means that the choice of employment is limited by the occupations carried on within the neighbourhood and, where the locality is highly specialized occupationally, this restriction may be severe. The Act therefore makes provision for those who have special aptitudes for which there is no scope locally to be placed in another area where they can be maintained and supervised whilst learning the trade for which they wish to qualify. It must be admitted that so far no very extensive use has been made of these powers probably because of the unwillingness of parents to allow their young sons and daughters to leave home so early in life; but the existence of the provision is in itself valuable in allowing opportunities for those who would otherwise find themselves too circumscribed.

II

A NEW DEAL

THE stimulus given by the Ministry of Labour to the formation of schemes for the orderly recruitment and training of young people after the war was not occasioned solely by concern for the skilled trades. It was part of a general realization that too little care had been given in the past to the channels by which school-leavers found their way into employment; and that in the future, with a rapidly falling adolescent population, it was urgently important to devise means for ensuring that youthful ability was not wasted. But the outcome of the movement then set on foot included a thorough overhaul of apprenticeship schemes in those industries which have a large proportion of skilled workers amongst their personnel.

The first step was taken in April, 1942, when at a meeting of the Joint Consultative Committee of representatives of the British Employers' Confederation and the Trades Union Congress, the Minister of Labour and National Service pointed out that in this country, unlike some others, there had been little development of pre-employment vocational training, and that few, if any, changes had been introduced into schemes of apprenticeship and learnership despite greatly expanded educational facilities for technical education offered by local education authorities during the present century. Already plans were being prepared for a thorough reorganization of the educational system—one which it was intended would include provision for the training of hand and eye which would be of great educational value irrespective of the means of livelihood which the young person entered. Moreover it was an integral part of the scheme of educational requirement that the school-leaving age should be raised to 15 and that, in addition, all those between this age and 18 should be released from employment for a day a week in order to attend educational classes. It was of course necessary to recognize that a very large proportion of young people, as of adults, must necessarily earn their living in occupations which require little technical skill or where formal technical instruction can provide only a small adjunct to the experience acquired by years of actual employment on the job. It was generally accepted that training in methods of production must be given in industry itself, but it was also held that workshop practice must be given in special educational institutions, particularly where skilled work is involved. The Government Departments—the Ministries of Labour and Education—believed that the main objective should be to go much farther than this and see that young people received the fullest opportunities to fit them for citizenship in a progressive community, by giving great attention to the cultural as well as technical education they received during adolescence. The County Colleges which it was hoped were later to be established for the further education of all young people were planned to include provision for liberal education as well as vocational. As far as the former was concerned, the Ministry of Education had much experience, but both it and the Ministry of Labour were anxious to obtain the advice and guidance of industry to ensure that the technical facilities provided within this wider framework should be in accordance with the changing needs of production.

It was decided at this joint meeting to single out certain industries which would be asked to consider a list of problems and give the Ministries the benefit of their considered replies. The questions were divided into those applying to youth in general, whatever the nature of the work in which they were engaged, and those applying principally to industries which required a period of apprenticeship. The first dealt with such matters as

(1) Should employers whose conditions of employment do

not comply with agreed conditions be allowed to employ juveniles?

(2) Should juveniles be restricted in their choice of jobs to employers complying with agreed conditions, and if so, up to what age should the restriction apply?

(3) Where progressive training is not practicable could extensive experience over a range of processes be arranged so that a young person could qualify for promotion?

(4) Should the State continue some measure of supervision after the completion of full-time education?

The second group asked:

(1) With whom should apprenticeship agreements be made:

    (*a*) an individual employer;

    (*b*) an employers' association;

    (*c*) a joint body?

(2) Should apprentices serve their time with more than one employer?

(3) How far should the improved standard of education of young people influence the period of apprenticeship?

(4) What reduction, if any, should be made in the period of apprenticeship for those who had had full-time pre-employment vocational training?

(5) Should Certificates of Competency be awarded and if so, by whom?

(6) Should Day Release for the purpose of technical training be extended, and made more systematic, and should it be made additional to the compulsory day-time release for continued education that was contemplated?

(7) How should a young person spend the interval between leaving school and entering industry?

Replies were received from a number of the industries to which the memorandum was sent and after discussion with further industrial representatives in the light of these replies the Joint Consultative Committee, in December, 1945, issued a Report on the Recruitment and Training of Juveniles in Industry which contained two important proposals. The first was that each industry be urged to establish agreed standards of employment for young workers and keep them continually under review through close collaboration between organized industry and the educational departments. It was urged that provision should be made in all industrial establishments for the appointment of qualified persons responsible for the recruitment and general well-being of the young workers, and in skilled trades where firms employed an appreciable number of apprentices, an Apprentice Supervisor should be appointed.

The second was that the Ministry of Labour should encourage in each main industry the establishment (if one did not already exist) of a National Joint Apprenticeship and Training Council to foster and supervise the introduction of training schemes in the firms within their scope.

The Report was widely circulated throughout industry and in order to encourage and assist industries in the preparation of their schemes the Ministry of Labour issued a Memorandum which made clear the fundamental principles that it believed should be kept in mind. The setting up of a national body representative of both sides in industry was felt to be a prime essential, but it was recognized that a national body could not maintain the close and continuous contact with individual firms that would be necessary if schemes were to be fully implemented, and the establishment of local joint bodies was therefore urged as an important element. The function of these bodies, both national and district, was to seek all means in their power to gain the adoption of the agreed training schemes by every individual firm in the industry. Although the final decision to engage any worker must necessarily be taken by the employer himself, recruitment through the Youth Employment Service was, it was urged, ultimately to the advantage of both employer and worker, and the closest co-operation between the Service and the joint body should therefore be maintained.

With regard to skilled occupations, careful selection, the Ministry insisted, is as essential as a carefully planned training programme. Young workers should be regarded more in the light of learners than of producers, and the aim of giving them as wide and comprehensive a knowledge of the trade as possible should take precedence over the contribution they might make to production during the training period. When a substantial period of training is involved a written indenture was encouraged, to which not only the young worker, his parent or guardian and the employer should be parties but also some further body representative of both sides in industry whose care it would be to ensure that the firm discharged its full responsibility to its trainees.

The response to this Memorandum was rather patchy. The immediate post-war period was one of major readjustment, as industries that had been swollen by war demands prepared to shrink to civilian proportions, and those that had been deliberately cut down to token size began the difficult process of retooling themselves and of attracting back the workers they had lost to the Forces and to munitions. After six years of war there were thousands of men coming back to civilian employment with no industrial experience or with experience that had grown rusty with disuse. Many men had gone straight into the Services after spending their adolescent years in unskilled or routine jobs, and now emerged in their early twenties with no obvious capacity that they could offer to an employer. There was no lack of available employment, rather the contrary, but these men had not the knowledge to enable them to be engaged without some preliminary training. Most industries were therefore, naturally enough, absorbed in this urgent and immediate problem of organizing short courses for adult trainees demobilized from the Forces, and could spare little time or thought to consider the much longer-term question of the right kind of provision for the training of young people for the future.

The Central Youth Employment Executive, which had been set up in April, 1946, in accordance with the recommendations of the Ince Committee, carried on negotiations with many national industrial organizations upon which it continually urged the acute need for greater attention to be given to this matter. As a result of this constant pressure, by 1950, fifty industries had agreed on their national schemes (and indeed it was not until 1955, that is, ten years after the publication of the Report of the Joint Consultative Committee that the hundred mark was at last reached), but even though schemes were agreed by national bodies there was no certainty that they had been implemented by the individual firms. Youth Employment Officers were urged to take the initiative in awakening local industries and trade unionists to the seriousness of the situation, and in order that they should be in a position to advise firms upon recruitment and training matters they were asked to make surveys of the arrangements already entered into by firms in their localities. In particular they were asked to discover the normal annual intake of young persons by local firms, the wages asked by adolescents, the methods of selection and training, and so on.

This information took considerably longer to collect than the C.Y.E.E. had hoped, partly no doubt because it coincided with the period of complete reorganization of the Youth Employment Service (mentioned in Chapter I) as a result of the Employment and Training Act of 1948. It took time for the educational authorities, which now became responsible for the organization of the young labour market in the majority of industrial areas, to work out their schemes and to staff their offices, and it took time again for the newly appointed Youth Employment Officers to learn sufficient of their local industries to enable them to make specific enquiries intelligently. It was not until 1952 therefore that the summary of reports made by the Youth Employment Committees on the basis of the surveys of the Youth Employment Officers became available.[1] These local surveys showed great extremes of development in the different industries and areas. Even in the industries in which national schemes had been formally established, the practical effect varied widely according to the attitude of the individual employer. Some had instituted elaborate well-thought-out schemes of supervision and training which were well in advance of the requirements of the national schemes; others, on the contrary, had no interest in the matter or even a definite prejudice against any change in the time-honoured methods of haphazard hiring or firing, and most disturbing of all, there were a great many who were entirely ignorant that any national scheme existed at all.

[1] C.Y.E.E. Memorandum No. 15.

Amongst those who had concerned themselves with the schemes there was again wide divergence with regard to the provision for further education, both in opinion and in practice. Some were strongly in favour of 'Day Release', that is, of paying their young workers for one day a week to attend formal instruction, but found it impossible to discover suitable educational facilities within reasonable travelling distances. Others believed that Day Release should be made conditional on the voluntary attendance by the young worker at evening classes, as only in this way could they feel confident that the day at the technical institute was not thought of simply as 'play time'. Some at the other extreme thought the whole business of formal instruction a bit of modern tomfoolery and that boys learn best on the job under the eye of the foreman. And just as the attitude of the employers varied, so too did that of the young workers themselves. As the County College section of the Education Act, 1944, has not yet been implemented, Day Release could rarely be offered for any other than technical instruction, and it was consequently only apprentices to skilled trades who were really concerned with this matter. Whilst there were many apprentices who welcomed the chance of learning something of the theoretical foundations of their work, there were many others who found it beyond their understanding, or who much resented the need to go back to school after they had become 'working men'.

Both the Ministry of Labour in its memorandum of guidance, and the majority of the national schemes based on it, had greatly stressed the importance of local machinery if the schemes were to be truly effective. Here again, the local surveys found much divergence in practice. In some areas, and in some industries, the local joint committees for apprenticeship and training were extremely active. Frequent meetings were held, and they exercised a marked influence in securing the observance of the nationally agreed schemes amongst the firms of the locality. In many, however, the local committees had not been set up, or else they met so infrequently that they were completely ineffective. Some committees indeed had so far misunderstood their functions as to consider it to be their primary duty to secure young recruits for local firms irrespective of their training arrangements or educational facilities.

It might at first sight seem surprising that in a period of full employment, when workers have the opportunity to pick and choose their jobs, industries which did not have any scheme of planned training or advancement for young workers should still have been able to draw upon a fair field. This was however the case. There were many enlightened firms which, even though they were in industries without national schemes, carefully planned and supervised the training and welfare of their young employees. But there were a larger number in which both employers and work-people were opposed to any essential change. Many young people and their parents showed themselves to be primarily interested in immediate money earnings, and were prepared to enter firms where piece work or bonus payment systems pushed up weekly earnings even though they offered nothing for the future. In the industries without accepted schemes there was, in particular, considerable opposition to the idea of Day Release for educational purposes. Many employers argued that it was too costly to pay wages to workers to go to school, and that in any case they should have finished their education during the extended school period, and not expect their employers to bear the brunt of a further period. Moreover the majority of them were fully convinced that a boy would learn much more of value in the factory than he would at school, and many boys and their parents were equally anxious not to forgo the higher earnings of a day on piece work for the time rate of pay got for a day at school.

The outcome of this rather disappointing survey was a decision to institute a more thorough examination of a selected number of industries which might enable more detailed information to be gained instead of these rather general impressions. On this it might be possible to consider the steps that could be effectively taken to extend and accelerate better arrangements. The industries chosen for this purpose, after consultation with their national associations, were engineering, printing, motor vehicle retail and repairing, boot and shoe manufacture, blacksmith, iron and steel. The Youth Employment Committees were asked to make an intensive examination of the firms in these industries in their areas and to provide details of the arrangements that existed for recruitment and training of young workers.

The picture emerging from the reports of the Youth Employment Officers all over the country was not much happier than the sketch provided by the earlier survey. In each of the industries examined the same comments continually appeared. But usually practice varied very greatly from firm to firm and region to region.

The arrangements in some firms were altogether admirable, with systematic training under the supervision of a specially appointed Apprentice Master, Day Release for all apprentices under 18 to attend technical instruction, and a demand for an approved standard of competence at the end. In others the situation was exactly the opposite. Nor was it apparently possible to make general observations about the categories in which the firms were likely to fall. On the whole the larger firms were more likely to be able to provide more carefully thought-out plans, but many small firms also did so, whilst on the contrary, many large firms still followed the old haphazard practice.

Day Release was not the general rule. Sometimes firms would have been willing to release their young workers if there had been adequate facilities in the neighbourhood, but often the local education authorities argued that facilities were not provided because so little use was made of them. Even amongst those firms that were prepared to release boys in localities where the facilities were available it seemed a fairly common practice to give boys time off only if they specifically asked for it, but not to make it an integral part of the apprentices' training.

For the most part the local organization of the schemes was hardly operative. Many areas had no committee, or if one existed in name it played a very slight part in the supervision of the actual work done by apprentices. And there were very few firms whose co-operation with the Youth Employment Officers was wholehearted. In some cases Y.E.O.s were invited to attend the meetings of Joint Apprenticeship Committees but firms generally recruited their apprentices direct. There were some few firms which made all their demands through the Y.E.O.s but they were a tiny minority. In printing and engineering, in particular, both of them very large industries, accounting for a high proportion of all apprentices, the potential supply of young workers eager to be apprentices was far in excess of the available vacancies, and as most large firms had a waiting list, there seemed to them no need to call on the Y.E.O.s for their help. In printing indeed the employers' policy was often directly contrary both to the clauses of the national scheme and to avowed educational policy, for they often insisted on young people taking up their apprenticeship at the particular moment a vacancy occurred, although this might mean that the boy had to leave school before finishing his course or sitting his examination. Thus a boy who decided to stay on at school found himself completely cut off from any chance of apprenticeship in this industry. One of the difficulties encountered in making the schemes effective was the existence of a large number of firms which were not members of the employers' association which had been a party to the agreement setting up the training scheme. Many of these firms remained ignorant of the existence of the schemes despite the efforts of the C.Y.E.E. and continued their old methods of recruitment entirely unaware that they had been urged to introduce any changes.

Meanwhile, however, uneasiness with regard to the future of industries depending on skilled workers was becoming more intense and more widespread. For the first few years after the end of the war it was easy to believe that manpower difficulties were caused by the shift over from a war to a peace basis of production. In the first year alone the Armed Forces which in June, 1945, had numbered well over 5 million dropped to little more than $1\frac{1}{2}$ million, with the corollary of a reduction in those employed in the manufacture of their equipment and supplies of a further 3 million. Not all of this latter group actually changed their jobs; many remained in the same firm, which, so to speak, was beating its swords into ploughshares and making civilian in the place of war goods.

But a very considerable proportion of this colossal figure of 6½ million was in fact moving from one type of employment to another, and this huge conversion seemed an adequate explanation of any difficulties in which large firms might find themselves in getting their staffs. By 1950, however, demobilization was complete, and the majority of firms had settled down into their peace-time pattern; and it was then that the fact had to be faced that not only was there a general manpower shortage but that the inadequacy of the supplies of skilled workers was acute. In the middle of that year the number of vacancies notified to the employment exchanges, but which they had been unable to fill, was 139,607 for men over the age of 18, and 55,447 for boys below that age. Of these the main manufacturing districts accounted for the largest proportions—London and the South-East for 31,135 men and 13,946 boys, the Midlands for 33,443 men and 12,698 boys, and the North-West for 17,465 men and 8,425 boys. At the same time the total of unemployed for the whole of Great Britain was only slightly above a quarter of a million, of whom one-third were not unemployed in any but the technical sense, i.e. they were in process of changing from one job to another and had had to register themselves for the short interval, generally of only one week and certainly of less than two.

In the following years the position changed hardly at all. The unemployment figure remained at the unprecedently low level of about 1·5% of the insured population and the numbers of unfilled vacancies for men kept somewhere about the 130,000–140,000 figure and for boys about 50,000. The shortage was serious at all levels and in all occupations, but its effects were particularly important amongst skilled workers in the basic industries because these so often represented the key jobs to a host of semi-skilled and unskilled processes. In the engineering and electrical industries, for example, there were in 1950 20,184 vacancies for skilled workers whilst under 2,000 names were registered as persons seeking work in these categories, and by 1955 the number of vacancies had increased to 30,870. In building, in 1950, there were 22,000 vacancies for skilled craftsmen—9,200 for bricklayers and

5,300 for painters amongst them—and five years later this total had risen to 28,450.[1]

This acute shortage of labour showed itself in the upward movement of wages. There is always some difficulty in making a comparison of wages at different times because of a number of factors. First, and most obviously, a change in money rates of pay is meaningless unless it is related to changes in retail prices; but quite apart from any judgment regarding the accuracy of the basis of calculation of the index used, a problem arises from the fact that the method of calculation and the fixing of the 'Base Year' have changed from time to time. Throughout the whole of the inter-war period, for example, the Base Year with which comparison was made was 1914. A new survey of household budgets was made in 1937/8 and this was intended to provide the material for a new 'Cost of Living Index'. Owing to the war however this was not introduced until 1947 and mid-June of that year became the new base with which comparisons were calculated. The 'Retail Price Index Figure' therefore shows the money that would be required at different dates to buy the same bundle of goods and services, and in the same proportions, as had been possible to purchase in June, 1947, for £100. Changes in rates of wages on the other hand are shown in relation to the position in 1938, so that one cannot simply compare the percentage movements in wages with the similar movements in prices since the starting points diverge so widely.

The second difficulty is that there is generally a wide discrepancy between wage rates and weekly earnings, which is accounted for by the regularity or otherwise of employment, by the amount of overtime worked, by the existence of piece rates and bonuses, and so on. If, for example, a trade union persuades employers to reduce the length of the normal working week, the effect is in fact the same as a rise in wages, for this means that whilst the same actual number of hours are worked, a higher proportion of them attract overtime pay. Thus earnings rise for the same amount of work though

---

[1] See Annual Reports, Ministry of Labour and National Service, for the appropriate years.

there has been no alteration in wage rates. In a period of buoyant markets and when the labour shortage is chronic, a great many 'extras' come to be added to wages—for night work or week-end work, for jobs that are less attractive than others, or simply as concealed bribes to act as magnets to attract workers where they are desperately needed. For these reasons earnings form a better standard of changes in remuneration than do wage rates.

By the middle of 1950 the earnings of adult men had risen by 118% in comparison with the last complete pre-war year. If however 1947 is taken as base so as to enable account to be taken of changes in retail prices the percentage increase was 22. At the same period the rise in prices was calculated to be 18%. Four years later the comparable figures were a rise of 60% in the earnings of adult men and of 44% for retail prices. It must be remembered that these earnings represent an average of all in manufacturing industries, including skilled, semi-skilled, and unskilled, those on fixed time rates and those on piece work, those in expanding industries and those in stationary or declining ones. They are given only as an indication of the trend.

Even more significant, however, was the movement in the earnings of young people, for this far outstripped that of adults. In 1950 the average earnings of boys and girls had risen 35% in comparison with 1947, in which year already they had risen to just over twice as high as they had been pre-war. By 1954 they had risen by 72% over the 1947 level; boys whose average weekly earnings in 1938 had been 26s. 1d. were getting £3 6s. 9d. in 1950 and £4 2s. in 1954. The competition for young recruits was becoming more and more intense and firms vied with one another in the amenities they offered to attract boys and girls to them—'Music While You Work', free lunch vouchers, welfare provisions of one sort or another, and so on.

For a good many years demographers had been forecasting the decrease in the number of those in the younger age groups which would characterize the 'forties and 'fifties of this century. The fall in the birth-rate which had been so important a factor of the present century was especially pronounced during the 'thirties and this meant an inevitable decline in the number of adolescents fifteen to eighteen years later. Added to this was the effect of the rise in the school-leaving age consequent upon the Education Act, 1944, which has resulted in there being only 'three years' worth' of young people available for employment (15–18 years) instead of four years' (14–18) as there had been before. From the last Census taken in the nineteenth century (1891) to that taken in 1951 the number of males in the population had risen by almost 50%, that is from 16 million to nearly $23\frac{1}{2}$ million, but the number of boys had gone up by only 400,000. Between 1931 and 1951 the number of adolescent boys (15–19 years of age) fell from 1,987,000 to 1,563,000 though the total number of males had risen during the same period by over two millions from 22,060,000 to 24,118,000. The gradual realization of the connection between the difficulties experienced by firms faced with a dearth of skilled workers, and the haphazard recruitment and training of the dwindling supply of young people, caused consternation over a wide field. One conference after another stressed the need for industries to set their houses in order and give more than lip service to schemes designed to ensure that young recruits were adequately trained to carry on their work.

There had been founded in 1919 an Association for Education in Industry and Commerce by a group of companies who felt strongly the need for some national organization to promote the education and training of employees. In the middle 'thirties this organization amalgamated with another whose purpose was similar—the British Association for Commercial Education—to form the British Association for Commercial and Industrial Education (B.A.C.I.E.). The funds for the maintenance of this body are provided by the member firms, by educational institutions, Government Departments and interested individuals, to enable the Association to keep the situation under constant review, as well as to provide information and advisory services to industry, and to organize courses to train personnel in charge of young workers. In the post-war period this Association's journal has referred again and again to the urgent need for the implementation by individual firms of the nationally agreed schemes for youth training, and has attempted, by giving details of schemes instituted by member firms, to encourage others to a similar development.

That an increasing number of firms and industries are operating training schemes is evidenced by the considerable number of boys who are apprenticed to a single craft or undergoing some form of learnership. In each of recent years over a quarter of a million boys between the ages of 15 and 17 have entered paid employment, and of these over 95,000 have been apprenticed to a craft or have been preparing for a recognized professional qualification (the figures do not distinguish between these two categories).[1] This is a considerably higher proportion than that of pre-war, when it was estimated that no more than one-fifth of young persons were receiving any form of systematic training.

Increased numbers undergoing training, while satisfactory in itself, is not enough to leave no cause for disquiet. There is still the question of whether the schemes themselves are adequate to the situation with which they have to deal. In practically all industries employing skilled workers, the apprenticeship schemes introduced by the national joint agreements have followed the same lines. Boys are accepted at the age of 16 with occasional provision made for a probationary period, in the year immediately after leaving school, in which suitability for training can be assessed; apprenticeship lasts five years during which those who are under 18 may be released from productive work at time wages, for a day a week, to attend technical classes, and the apprentice reaches adult status and adult wages at the age of 21. In some cases full-time attendance at technical secondary school is allowed to shorten the period of apprenticeship by six months or a year. But as, on the whole, the full five years are demanded, it is difficult, if not entirely impossible, for boys to be accepted for apprenticeship after the age of 16–17. In some schemes the first year of apprenticeship training is designed so as to be a common basis for

[1] Reports of the National Youth Employment Council and the *Ministry of Labour Gazette*.

several crafts and at the end of this year the boy and his employer can choose to which branch he should henceforward be attached. But having made the choice at this time he continues to specialize further and further in the same field and is not allowed at a later age to move from one craft to another.

The rigidity of these schemes now became a matter of comment. It seemed difficult to believe that by some curious coincidence every craft, whatever its nature, requires five years of training, or that young men are incapable of learning after the age of 21. It sometimes happens that boys, when they first leave school, are dazzled by the prospect of higher earnings in semi-skilled or unskilled occupations, or that the domestic circumstances of the family necessitate that earnings should be as high as possible at once. Later however the boy will have had more opportunity to gain experience of the industrial world, or perhaps the domestic situation has eased, and he may be eager to prepare himself for skilled work. It seemed to many critics both uneconomic from the point of view of productive efficiency, and unjust from the point of view of the individual, that a choice made at the age of 15–16 should be binding for the rest of a man's life.

Moreover educational facilities have vastly increased since the traditional period of apprenticeship became established. Did it not seem at least probable that more highly educated boys could master the work in a shorter period of time than had previously been required? And with the technical instruction available might not the possibility present itself of enabling a boy to train in two or more crafts during his period of apprenticeship, and thus provide both himself and industry with a degree of flexibility in the use of skill that at the moment is impossible. Flexibility, indeed, had become one of the prime needs, for many firms were continually finding themselves in difficulties as work was held up and both skilled and semi-skilled men in one branch of the work were compelled to be idle because of the bottleneck caused by lack of trained persons in some other part. If men could be allowed to move rather more freely from one type of work to another which was fairly closely allied to it the work of all might become more regular and the flow of production be more even.

One of the main effects therefore of the acute shortage of skilled workers was to change somewhat the emphasis in the desire to provide for better training of the young. It had begun primarily with the aim of preventing the wastage of young lives and abilities and in the hope that if more care were taken at the outset of industrial life there would be fewer social casualties later on. It developed during the war from a generous determination to give young people a better chance than they had had in the past, not only as recruits to the industrial army, but as future citizens of the community. The schemes for the training of young workers encouraged by the Ministry of Labour and the C.Y.E.E. were intended to provide opportunities for those engaged in semi-skilled or unskilled operations to get the kind of supervised, varied experience that might fit them for promotion as well as for the training of craftsmen. In both categories great emphasis was laid on the need for welfare amenities and the industrial training schemes were intended to link up with the re-organization of the educational system by allowing young workers whether skilled or not to be free for one day a week to attend the County Colleges that it was hoped would be established. But the difficulties with which industries were faced owing to the lack of an adequate supply of skilled workers brought into greater prominence questions connected with the methods employed by industries—even those that were implementing agreed schemes—to select and train their future skilled workers. How far were these schemes adequate to cope with the situation? Were workers trained in the best and most constructive methods? Could the period of training be reduced, and if so, by how much? Was, in fact, a radical change in attitude needed?

It was with such questions in mind that the National Joint Advisory Council of the Ministry of Labour decided to invite some industries to review their training schemes,[1] and in particular to consider:

(*a*) Whether the scope of training arrangements could be widened.

---

[1] *Ministry of Labour Gazette*, February, 1952.

(*b*) Whether the period of training could be shortened.

(*c*) Whether the minimum age of entry into apprenticeship should be lowered.

(*d*) Whether the upper age limit should be either removed or modified to allow older workers who had shown themselves potentially suitable to be accepted as craft apprentices.

(*e*) Whether with intensive methods of training workers could be trained for a wider range of employment.

No quick reply to such questions could be expected, for they involve a fundamental change in the way in which most people have come to look upon training problems. Great Britain has such a long tradition of skilled workmanship that the regulations concerning apprenticeship have acquired almost the force of a natural law and are very rarely questioned or criticized. This makes it much more difficult to envisage a complete reshaping of training schemes. In the U.S.A., on the other hand, there has not until recently been any need for specific provision for training skilled workers. American industry has been able to rely on a constant flow of skilled men from European countries, and it is only since the severe restrictions of immigration became effective that industry there has had to face the fact that provision must be made for training, in particular, in those occupations in which a high degree of trained skill is required. Starting with, as it were, a clean sheet, has allowed America to experiment with such things as adult apprenticeship with training primarily at a technical school instead of in the works, and with apprenticeship to an industry instead of to an individual firm, because there was little organized resistance to such innovations. The older skilled workers who might have been opposed to them came from many different countries with varying traditions of apprenticeship. In England, on the contrary, both employers and trade unions have grown up in the same traditional pattern and are inclined to take it as sacrosanct that apprentices are always adolescents between the ages of 16 and 21, that it takes five years to learn a skilled trade, that one learns only one trade and sticks to that, and that most of one's training must be done on the job. Any reorganization, therefore, is as much concerned with the institutional and psychological factors in skilled industry as with the practical problems of the methods of training that might be successfully introduced.

III

THE METHOD OF THE ENQUIRY

THE aim of the present enquiry is to try to find the answers to a number of questions. First and foremost, what are the reasons for the continuing shortage of skilled workers? Is this due, for example, to the unwillingness of some firms in each industry to take their quota of training responsibility, or are firms restricted in the number of trainees they can admit, and if so, is this number inadequate to meet the needs of the industry? Is the difficulty perhaps due to faulty selection so that a considerable number of those who begin apprenticeship fail to stay the course and leave before becoming qualified? What proportion of those who serve their full term proceed later to some form of work other than that for which they have qualified? During the post-war period it is known that wage differentials between skilled and semi-skilled workers have materially narrowed, and in some cases the semi-skilled worker on piece rates can earn actually more than the skilled craftsman. Has this narrowing of differentials reduced the attractions of apprenticeship with the result that the numbers applying are insufficient, or does it induce skilled workers, once qualified, to change over to semi-skilled jobs?

How could the shortage be reduced? Would it be possible to shorten the period of training? Could apprenticeship be opened to suitable adults employed in semi-skilled operations? Could apprentices be trained for more than one craft so that with a more mobile and flexible labour force bottlenecks in a particular branch of production might be prevented?

Answers to these questions demand investigations along

two lines. There is first the factual situation. What in practice happens? Are agreed schemes being implemented, and if not, where does the deficiency show itself? Are the agreed schemes inadequate to meet the need, and if not, what changes in them would be technically possible? The second, and in one sense the more fundamental problem, is concerned with the way in which people in the industry look at the matter. If it were technically possible to train an apprentice in, say, three or four years instead of five, are there difficulties in the way of introducing such a change? There is the Trade Union attitude, for example, to the introduction of adult apprentices or to training a boy for more than one branch of work that must be considered. And if there are difficulties could these be overcome?

It is only necessary to list questions of this kind for it to become obvious that the answers to them could not be got without preliminary and intensive enquiry over a wide field. At first the possibility suggested itself of an intensive investigation on a very narrow front—for example, the training schemes and the attitudes to them in one or two firms. But interesting as such an enquiry might have been from many points of view it would not have helped in any way to answer the questions asked. The earlier enquiries carried out by the Ministry of Labour and the Youth Employment Service showed conclusively the wide divergence that exists in practice between the firms in an industry which have complex and elaborate training schemes and others in the same occupational field, and often in the same locality, which remain in ignorance that there are any schemes in existence at all. The conclusion therefore had to be drawn that detailed knowledge of the operations of one or two firms would not allow any valid generalization to be made.

The decision therefore was taken to make a more general enquiry covering as wide a field as possible, and little consideration is needed to show that the wider the scope the more difficult it must be to get accurate information. In the previous surveys made, the Ministry of Labour with its nation-wide network of regional and local offices had been unable to get more than documented general impressions.

These impressions were valuable as giving some indication of the general coverage of training schemes, and of the extent to which firms were attempting to put national agreements into operation. They did not even attempt to do more than this, and their results consequently could not provide a firm basis for any further action except continued encouragement along the same lines. But if a Government Department, with offices in every area and with officials in constant contact with firms, was unable to get detailed information, a single individual with very modest resources is unlikely to be more successful. It was necessary therefore to compromise by concentrating the enquiry on what was likely to be the most fruitful field whilst making it wide enough to offer a firm foundation for generalization.

The outstanding characteristic of industry in the twentieth century is the spread of mass-production methods; more and more skilled jobs have been subdivided into their constituent processes, each of which can be taken over by machinery, operated by workers whose activities are confined to the repetition of one narrow range of actions. The great majority of workers are now semi-skilled and require little more training in these operations than could be acquired in periods ranging from a few days to a few weeks. But the degree to which repetition methods can be introduced into industry is not the same in all types of production; it depends partly on the technical possibilities and partly on the size of the accessible market. The specialization of tools and operations to perform a particular process is worth-while only if the finished product is wanted in large enough quantities and over a sufficiently long period to justify the investment. A machine can repeat an operation more quickly and more accurately than a man; it does the same thing over and over again without tiring and can be relied upon to repeat itself with unfailing precision. But the point is that it does the *same* thing over and over again and cannot be changed except within comparatively narrow limits. Thus it is only if a large number of identical articles is required that mass production is economical, and the size of the market for such identical goods depends on such factors as taste (the demand for standard household equipment is larger than that for fashion clothes) or education (there is a larger market for the popular magazine than for the learned journal) or convenience (the retail store for groceries must be close to homes, and its customers are limited to those living in the neighbourhood, but the piano store could serve a wide area because it is worth travelling a few miles to buy something that one gets only once in a lifetime) or transportability (heavy or bulky articles are too expensive to carry over a long distance, and unless their value is very high, costs of transport counterbalance economies in mass production).

The proportion of skilled workers needed in any industry varies, therefore, according to the degree by which mass production methods can be introduced. Houses which must be built on the site they are to occupy offer fewer opportunities than the manufacture of pins, for example. The great advantage of the skilled worker is that he can apply his knowledge and trained manipulative dexterity to a succession of jobs whilst the semi-skilled worker can only repeat the same process.

In every industry and in every firm a nucleus of skilled workers is essential. Machines have to be set and maintained for the semi-skilled workers to operate and almost invariably there are one or two processes which, while an essential ingredient in the final product, do not justify investment in expensive machinery. But the proportion of the labour force included in this nucleus varies widely from one industry to another. There are unfortunately no figures published which enable one to calculate accurately the proportions of skilled, semi-skilled and unskilled in each industry. The occupational categories in the Census are not divided along this line, but some idea of the relative importance of skilled workers can be gained from a study of the jobs into which young people go on leaving school.

In 1952 63,000 of the 267,000 boys who left school between the ages of 15 and 17 became apprentices or learners in skilled crafts. Of these 23·4% entered the engineering, shipbuilding and electrical goods industries, 20·6% entered building and contracting, 13·7% the vehicle industry, and 3·6%

47

printing. Although the last-named is so much smaller a proportion of the total than the others, it yet represents almost half of the young people entering that industry, with the exception of those in clerical employment, but the industry itself accounts for only 2·3% of the insured population in contrast to engineering, shipbuilding and electrical[1] industries which account for 8·8%, vehicles for 5·1% and building for 5·5%. Even so the proportion of apprentices is less in printing than in these other industries. In engineering 66% of boys between 15 and 17, other than those in clerical employment, become apprentices and journeymen, in vehicles 62% and in building,[2] nearly 72%.

No other industries come anywhere near to the proportion of these groups, and only one or two approach the position in printing.

For these reasons it was decided to confine the enquiry to engineering, shipbuilding, the motor repair industry, printing, and building, since these between them account for by far the largest number of skilled workers.

The enquiry is confined to male apprentices since the number of skilled women workers is comparatively small, and particularly so in the group of industries chosen. In engineering, shipbuilding and electrical goods, there were only 350 girl apprentices between 15 and 17 out of a total of 11,490 entering the industry; in vehicles only 86 out of 4,407; in printing 728 out of 8,757 and in building 64 out of 2,049. In industry as a whole there were only 14,000 girl apprentices out of a total of more than a quarter of a million entering employment (256,000) and the only two occupations with any considerable number of them were the clothing trades (3,960) and the distributive trades (2,096).

The smallness of these numbers is the result of the broken term of industrial life which is usual amongst women. Practically all girls work for wages when they leave school, but it is usual for them to leave employment when they marry or, at least, on the birth of the first baby. In the past their exit from industry has been permanent with the exception of the

[1] *Ministry of Labour Gazette,* 1955.
[2] *Ibid.,* December, 1953.

small number who became widows or who were deserted by their husbands while they were still in the working age group. Before the war only one-ninth of all married women were in any form of paid employment and a very large number were not in industry but were supplementing their husband's inadequate incomes by office cleaning, charing, or other forms of part-time domestic work. Since the war the proportion has risen steeply and now one-fifth of all married women work for pay, but most do not do so without interruption. The vast majority of girls marry young, in the early twenties, and even though it is no longer universal for the break with industry to be permanent, most retire from paid work for at least a considerable number of years whilst they are looking after their young families. It is not considered worth the while of most employers therefore to spend resources on training workers who will leave the industry just about the time that they become fully qualified. Nor is this restriction resented by the girls or by their parents. In the past parents have found the support of a child during apprenticeship a fairly heavy burden which they have been willing to bear only for the sake of the future benefit of the boy who becomes firmly established as a skilled craftsman. Such a drain on the family exchequer seemed an unnecessary sacrifice on behalf of a daughter whose whole industrial life would probably last no more than about ten years. Even if parents had been willing to make the sacrifice very few girls were anxious to take advantage of any such opportunities offered to them. To most girls leaving school it has seemed foolish to train for five years at a small wage for a job which one was unlikely to practise. Semi-skilled work at much better wages than apprentices could earn allowed one to buy clothes and hair-perms, to go to the cinema and dance-halls, and to take part in all those activities which were most likely to lead to the altar. With the exception of certain branches of the clothing, and some of the domestic trades—both types of work which would be useful after marriage—there has never been more than a smattering of skilled women workers employed; nor any serious demand on the part of women wage earners to alter this situation. It may be that this may change radically in the future as a result of the trend to early marriage and small families. The large majority of families are completed within the first decade of marriage, most of them within the first five years, and this means that by the early forties most women are free of their heaviest domestic responsibilities while they have still twenty or twenty-five years of full activity before them. The effect of this is already seen in the much larger number of married women who now return to industry when their children are old enough to go to school. This may perhaps lead to a greater willingness in the future to train for skilled work with the idea of returning to wage-earning after a period of purely domestic activity. At present however this has not begun to operate, and the enquiry has therefore been confined to boy apprentices.

The industries selected employ between them nearly half of all men engaged in the manufacturing industries, with the addition of building. They are widely dispersed over the country, though concentrated more in some areas than in others—engineering, for example, in the Midlands, printing in the Home Counties, shipbuilding on Tyneside, Clydeside, Southampton and so on. With the exception of the shipbuilding industry, they contain firms of every size from the tiny business to the giant, and even shipbuilding includes boatbuilders, the majority of which are firms of a small size.

The Census of Production 1948 provides the latest available figures of the structure of industry and its geographical distribution. From this one can compile tables showing:

(*a*) the number of firms in the industry in each of the eleven regional areas in which the country is divided by the Ministry of Labour and National Service, and

(*b*) the number of firms falling within each size group reckoned by the number of persons employed.

For the selected industries this gives the following results:

I. PRINTING

(a) *Area Distribution*		(b) *Size Distribution*	
Area	No. of establishments	No. employed	No. of establishments
Northern Counties	83	1–10	3,272
E. and W. Ridings	200	11–24	961
N. Midlands	162	25–49	681
E. Counties	130	50–99	399
London and S.E. Counties	867	100–199	216
Southern Counties	102	200–299	57
S.W. Counties	111	300–399	31
Midlands	191	400–499	16
N.W. Counties	314	500–749	19
Wales	31	750–999	8
Scotland	207	1,000–1,499	6
		1,500+	4

II. BUILDING

(a) *Area Distribution*		(b) *Size Distribution*	
Area	No. of establishments	No. employed	No. of establishments
Northern Counties	3,741	1–10	57,184
N.E. Counties	6,669	11–50	13,321
N. Midlands	5,549	51–99	1,790
E. Counties	5,536	100–499	1,263
London	12,698	500+	171
Southern Counties	4,415		
S.W. Counties	5,430		
Midlands	5,764		
N.W. Counties	8,830		
S.E. Counties	4,583		
Wales	3,160		
Scotland	7,554		

III. MOTOR VEHICLE RETAIL AND REPAIR

(a) Area Distribution			(b) Size Distribution	
Area	No. of establishments		No. employed	No. of establishments
Northern Counties	1,141		1–4	13,193
E. and W. Ridings	1,770		5–9	6,835
N. Midlands	1,935		10–24	3,881
E. Counties	1,933		25–49	1,518
London and S.E. Counties	5,399		50–99	685
Southern Counties	1,782		100–199	293
S.W. Counties	2,024		200–499	185
Midlands	2,551		500–999	71
N.W. Counties	2,751		1,000–1,499	28
Wales	1,052		1,500+	45
Scotland	1,959			

IV. ENGINEERING (i) MECHANICAL ENGINEERING

(a) Area Distribution			(b) Size Distribution	
Area	No. of establishments		No. employed	No. of establishments
Northern Counties	144	*General*	1–10	3,042
E. and W. Ridings	378		11–24	771
N. Midlands	241		25–49	647
E. Counties	195		50–99	511
London and S.E. Counties	923		100–199	352
Southern Counties	135		200–299	143
S.W. Counties	176		300–399	89
Midlands	484		400–499	58
N.W. Counties	505		500–749	74
Wales	76		750–999	46
Scotland	334		1,000–1,499	31
			1,500–1,999	17
			2,000+	26
		Repairing	1–10	832
			11–24	447
			25–49	240
			50–99	92
			100–199	36
			200–299	5
			300–749	6

IV. ENGINEERING (ii) IRON AND STEEL

(a) *Area Distribution*		(b) *Size Distribution*	
Area	No. of establishments	No. employed	No. of establishments
Northern Counties	39	1–49	144
E. and W. Ridings	140	50–99	63
N. Midlands	16	100–499	143
London, S.E. and			
E. Counties	10	500–999	35
Midlands	77	1,000–1,499	13
N.W. Counties	33	1,500–2,999⎱	40
		3,000+ ⎰	
Wales	33		
Scotland	50		

IV. ENGINEERING (iii) IRON FOUNDRIES

(a) *Area Distribution*		(b) *Size Distribution*	
Area	No. of establishments	No. employed	No. of establishments
Northern Counties	49	1–49	591
E. and W. Ridings	119	50–99	195
N. Midlands	85	100–399	209
E. Counties	30	400+	70
London and S.E.			
Counties	40		
Southern Counties	17		
S.W. Counties	21		
Midlands	239		
N.W. Counties	136		
Wales	32		
Scotland	102		

53

IV. ENGINEERING (iv) ELECTRICAL ENGINEERING

(a) Area Distribution		(b) Size Distribution	
Area	No. of establishments	No. employed	No. of establishments
Northern Counties	31	1–10	972
E. and W. Ridings	71	11–24	219
N. Midlands	39	25–49	203
E. Counties	46	50–99	165
London and S.E. Counties	323	100–199	96
Southern Counties	30	200–299	51
S.W. Counties	35	300–399	27
Midlands	134	400–499	24
N.W. Counties	103	500–749	28
Wales	31	750–999	22
Scotland	49	1,000–1,499	26
		1,500+	31

V. SHIPBUILDING AND REPAIRING (*including Boatbuilding*)

(a) Area Distribution		(b) Size Distribution	
Area	No. of establishments	No. employed	No. of establishments
Northern Counties	80	1–49	649
E. and W. Ridings	42	50–99	120
N. Midlands	27	100–199	95
E. Counties	39	200–299	35
London and S.E. Counties	127	300–399	29
Southern Counties	50	400–499	13
S.W. Counties	34	500–749	38
Midlands	6	750–999	18
N.W. Counties	84	1,000–1,499	15
Wales	40	1,500–2,499 ⎫	
		2,500–4,999 ⎬	36
Scotland	149	5,000+ ⎭	

It was decided to select not more than 1,000 firms chosen so as to represent a fair sample by size and district of these industries. It was anticipated, as in fact proved to be the case, that there would be serious difficulties encountered in

getting detailed information by means of a postal questionnaire and that it would be necessary to supplement this by
personal interviews. This being so, lack of resources made it
essential to keep the sample to a minimum, particularly in
view of the wide dispersal of firms over the whole of Great
Britain. Personal interviews thus involved a considerable
amount of travelling, and even with the greatest readiness
to co-operate on the part of the firms concerned, it is not
always possible for a large number of firms in the same area
to be able to give time during the same few days to answer
enquiries. At the outset of the enquiry a good deal of apprehension was felt on the score of the comparative smallness
of the samples, but as it developed, this fear disappeared.
The same situation was found to exist so often amongst firms
in similar circumstances, and the reactions of employers and
trade unionists seemed so often to follow a general pattern
that it is at least probable that a larger number of firms in
the sample would merely have confirmed the results obtained.

The number of firms taken as an appropriate sample of
each industry, or for a clearly marked sub-section of an industry, varied from a minimum of 69 in Iron and Steel to a
maximum of 202 in General Engineering.

Printing Industry	101	firms
Building Industry	150	,,
Motor Vehicle Retail and Repair	146	,,
Engineering (Mechanical)	202	,,
,, (Iron and Steel)	69	,,
,, (Iron Foundry)	70	,,
,, (Electrical)	86	,,
Shipbuilding and Boatbuilding	99	,,

It was intended that the number of firms selected should
reflect the regional distribution of the total population of
firms in that industry, e.g. if half the total number of firms
in an industry fell in the size group 1–10 employees, then
out of a sample of 100 firms, 50 would be chosen from that
group. Further, if one-third of the total number of firms in
the country were situated in the London and South-East
Region, then out of the 100 firms, 33 would be selected from
that area. This has not however always proved possible. The

lists of firms from which a sample could be drawn, their size and location, have been made after consultation of classified industrial directories, and after prolonged discussions with the appropriate employers' associations and Government Departments. The actual firm included in the sample was the result of a random selection from the particular size group or the geographical region, but whereas in some cases it was possible to get accurate figures about both size and location of firms in the industry or sub-section, in some, information about size alone was available, and in others, about situation alone. Where in such circumstances a random selection showed an undue preponderance of one particular category, another firm was later substituted so as to get a sample which corresponded as closely as possible to the structure and siting of the industry as shown by the Census of Production.

The sample finally decided upon was as follows:

I. BUILDING

No. of employees	No. of firms
1–10	30
11–30	18
31–50	13
51–99	18
100–249	19
250–499	14
500–999	13
1,000–4,999	18
5,000+	7
	150

From the following districts:

Area	No. of firms
Greater London	39
S., S.W., S.E.	25
Midlands and N. Midlands	42
Scotland	18
E. Counties	9
N.E. Counties	9
Wales	8
	150

II. MOTOR VEHICLE RETAIL AND REPAIR

No. of employees	No. of firms
1–4	49
5–9	49
10–24	26
25–49	10
50–99	5
100–199	3
200–499	2
500–999	1
1,000 +	1
	146

From the following districts:

Area	No. of firms
London and S.E.	32
Devon, Cornwall, W., S.W. and S. Counties	24
Cumberland, Westmorland, Yorks, N. and N.E. Counties	33
Lancs., Cheshire, Midlands and E. Counties	39
Scotland	12
Wales	6
	146

III. PRINTING

No. of employees	No. of firms
1–10	55
11–24	16
25–49	12
50–99	7
100–199	3
200–749	4
750 +	4
	101

Taken from the following districts:

Area	No. of firms
London and S.E. Counties	56
N. Counties	3
Yorkshire	9
N. Midlands	7
E. Counties	5
S. Counties	4
S.W. Counties	5
Midlands	9
N.W. Counties	13
Wales	1
Scotland	9
	101

IV. SHIPBUILDING AND SHIP-REPAIRING
(*including Boatbuilding*)

No. of employees	No. of firms
1–49	22
50–99	10
100–199	7
200–299	6
300–399	7
400–499	5
500–749	16
750–999	7
1,000–1,499	6
1,500–2,499	6
2,500–4,999	5
5,000+	2
	99

Taken from the following districts:

Area	No. of firms
North	14
Yorkshire	7
Midlands and East	9
London and S.E.	13
South and S.W.	24
North-West	2
Wales	5
Scotland	24
N. Ireland	1
	99

V. IRON AND STEEL

No. of employees	No. of firms
1–49	13
50–99	10
100–499	27
500–999	7
1,000–1,499	3
1,500–2,999	3
3,000+	6
	69

Taken from the following districts:

Area	No. of firms
Yorkshire, Derbyshire	24
S. Wales and Monmouthshire	15
Midland Counties	12
N. Counties	8
Scotland	7
Lancs. and N.W. Counties	3
	69

VI. IRON FOUNDRY

No. of employees	No. of firms
1–49	37
50–99	11
100–399	10
400+	12
	70

Area	No. of firms
London and S.E. Counties	6
Central Midlands	20
N. Midlands and Derbyshire	20
N. and N.W. Counties	15
Scotland	9
	70

VII. ENGINEERING

(a) General

Area	No. of firms
N. Counties	8
Yorkshire	25
London and S. Counties	58
S.W. Counties	7
Midlands and E. Counties	56
N.W. Counties	27
Wales	2
Scotland	19
	202

(b) Electrical

Area	No. of firms
London and S. Counties	38
Midlands	20
Lancs. and N.W. Counties	10
N.E. Counties	14
Scotland	4
	86

In the engineering industry there was not the necessary information about the size of firms, and selection had to be made on a geographical basis.

Before deciding on the form the enquiry should take, many visits were paid to employers' associations, to trade unions and to individual firms in order to establish the type of question to which it might be possible to get definite answers. It soon became apparent that any printed questionnaire would have to be stripped to the barest essentials, partly because of the intimidating effect on a harassed employer or works manager of the sight of a long list of questions, even if the answers, once he had brought himself to read the questions, were easy to supply; but much more because of the difference in the practice of firms in the ways in which records are kept. Again naturally enough firms keep records only of those matters which are likely to be useful to them in their own work, and not to provide answers to the questions of the social investigator. Thus experience showed that certain parts of the enquiry had to be reluctantly abandoned. It was not possible, for example, to find out how many apprentices when qualified left the craft for which they had trained and went into other work which offered them higher remuneration, since there is no reason for firms to keep records of the subsequent industrial history of those who leave them. Many of those who left after finishing their term of apprenticeship probably went as skilled workers to other firms, but probably also, many others left the industry entirely. The records made it impossible to distinguish.

On the basis of pilot enquiries conducted by personal interviews a printed questionnaire was prepared (see Appendix), and circulated to the firms selected for the sample. A considerable number of replies was received within a short period, many of them showing that firms had obviously devoted a great deal of care to giving accurate information. After a follow-up letter a further batch of replies was received.

Correspondence with firms that had not replied at all showed:

(*a*) that the reason a number had not filled up the questionnaire was not because they were unwilling to co-operate but because they did not know how to adjust their records to the questions asked, and

(*b*) that a fairly large number had thought it to be no concern of theirs because they did not employ any apprentices at all. This second point was particularly important because one of the main objects of the enquiry was to determine whether there was any large proportion of firms that employed skilled workers but did not train them, and when this answer was returned, firms were asked to give simply the number of adult workers employed and the number of skilled men amongst them. To cope with the first difficulty a very large number of personal interviews were arranged and the answers to the questions inserted during the interviews. In all, 550 answers were obtained, distributed amongst the industries as follows:

Printing Industry	67
Building Industry	92
Motor Vehicle Industry	97
Shipbuilding and Boatbuilding Industry	49
Engineering (Mechanical)	120
,, (Iron and Steel)	47
,, (Iron Foundries)	36
,, (Electrical)	42

It will be seen therefore that the information obtained from this questionnaire cannot be considered to have statistical accuracy and significance. The size of the sample is not sufficiently large, and the answers covered only 60% of those to whom the questionnaire was sent. What it does do, however, is to give a fairly clear indication of the position, and to bring out certain features very distinctly. In addition, it has given an opportunity to discuss the matter very fully with those most intimately concerned, and thus provided material on which to judge how far changes in the system seem likely or possible.

IV

THE SCHEMES IN OPERATION

ALTHOUGH the apprentice schemes now in operation have many family features in common there are sufficient variations for it to be worth while to outline each individually, particularly so because, in certain cases, the variations are the result of the historical and technical developments of the industry concerned.

ENGINEERING AND SHIPBUILDING

Engineering is not one industry but a large group of related activities, and it is difficult to know where to draw any dividing line. Mechanical engineering, marine engineering, shipbuilding, electrical engineering, iron foundries and iron and steel manufacturing are separate industries, but they overlap so much that it is almost impossible to know where one begins and another ends. A great many firms carry out several types of production and think of themselves as members of one or other branch of the engineering industry, sometimes according to their dominant interest and sometimes according to the subject under discussion. It is indicative of this that the Ministry of Labour statistics with regard to manpower, etc., almost always list the whole group together as 'engineering, shipbuilding and electrical industries'. In official statistics this group is separated from those comprising 'metal manufacturing', of which iron and steel and iron foundries are the principals; but here again, the lines of demarcation are so blurred and so many engineering firms are concerned with those types of work that it has been decided to include them in this group of activities.

When the Amalgamated Society of Engineers was founded in 1851, those entitled to membership were all skilled men—engineers, machinists, smiths, millwrights, patternmakers—and for three-quarters of a century the policy of the Union was mainly dictated by the effort to preserve the status and pay of skilled men in the face of rapid changes in industrial techniques. Hardly a year passed without the introduction of some new method which either greatly speeded up the work done by the skilled men, or, more often, enabled such a sub-division and simplification of a skilled process that the job could be undertaken by semi-skilled operatives. The two chief methods by which engineers sought to protect themselves were, firstly, by trying to establish lines of demarcation which marked off certain territories of work as the sole prerogative of the skilled man, and secondly, by regulating the entry to the trade.

In the early years of the Union's existence 'one boy to four men' was the standard aimed at, but it remained a hope rather than a reality. In the 'eighties when the depression, that was to last until the turn of the century, was just beginning, and the large amount of unemployment amongst engineers brought this matter to the forefront of discussion, it was stated that sons were being signed on as apprentices to do the jobs from which their fathers had been sacked. The Sunderland branch of the Union, which was the spearhead of the fight at that time, collected figures to show that in one local works there were 23 journeymen with 37 apprentices, and in another there were 54 apprentices to only 25 adult men. In seven of the leading firms taken together, there were nearly 500 apprentices out of a total employment of 1,200. The union urged that it was essential to limit the number of apprentices so that there should be no more than 1 to every 2 journeymen, and the men felt so strongly on this matter that they came out on strike and remained out at very great sacrifice. But the depression defeated them and they were forced to go back without gaining their point.

As long as the skill required for jobs remained high the

power of employers to use the less qualified worker was strictly limited, and it was not until big developments in machine production had taken place that the right insisted on by the employers 'to select and train their workers' provided a serious challenge to the pay and status of the skilled men. The Union argued that a man who had given years of his life to master a craft should have a right to preferential employment and that it was unjust to take on untrained handymen whilst skilled workers were out of a job. Many skilled men refused to show the new operatives what they had to do, or to supervise their work, on the ground that if the employer said it was his right to select and train any men he liked, he could do it himself without their assistance. But they were fighting a losing battle. The semi-skilled men were completely unorganized and could be taken on at rates which were very little above those earned by labourers. It was unlikely that employers would agree to retain the system by which certain types of work were the monopoly of members of a union, to which a five-year apprenticeship was a condition of entry, when the skill required to do the job was such as could be mastered in a comparatively short time by men willing to do the work at lower rates. A minority of the Union recognized the logic of events and argued that

> 'instead of wasting time and energy in putting forward sentimental reasons why tradesmen should be allowed to man certain machine tools, we should make the conditions of entry into our Society easier . . . and so get all the workers in the engineering industry, both skilled and semi-skilled, into the A.S.E.' [1]

But only a small proportion of the members supported this view, and the union continued with its traditional policy.

A revolutionary change in the situation came, however, with the outbreak of the first World War. The need to increase enormously and quickly the output of munitions whilst, at the same time, releasing all available manpower for the Forces necessitated a different attitude to demarcation questions and the problems regarding the relationship of skilled

---

[1] Jefferies, *The Story of the Engineers*, p. 157.

and semi-skilled workers. The majority of men in the engineering industry supported the war and were willing, for patriotic reasons, to give up their opposition to restrictive practices which they would otherwise have continued to maintain; but they did so on condition that the Government and the employers pledged themselves to restore the traditional practices when the emergency was over. In this way much of the work that had formerly been considered the monopoly of skilled men was thrown open to much less highly qualified workers. Semi-skilled men were upgraded to do jobs that had been listed as skilled, and women were introduced in large numbers to take on the purely repetition processes. Not all the men acquiesced in these agreements, and throughout the war there were constant strikes which were often as much against the men's own union leaders as against employers. Despite this internal dissension the war gave a great impetus to organization, and the membership of the A.S.E. increased by nearly 80% during these years; but the great changes in techniques that the war had accelerated brought the recognition that the scope of the Union no longer fitted the situation, and almost immediately after the end of the war, in 1920, the Amalgamated Engineering Union came into existence as an amalgamation of several bodies catering for closely allied branches of engineering work.

The new Union was not as comprehensive as its supporters had hoped, for their ambition had been to include within one association every type of skilled metal worker with the exception of those engaged in the actual making of iron and steel; but the Iron Founders and the Boiler Makers and some other Unions refused to enter the new association. By this amalgamation the A.E.U. lost the strict craft basis that had been the character of the A.S.E., for it admitted within its membership many grades of worker who could not be called skilled. A further widening of its scope took place when it associated with other organizations to form the Confederation of Shipbuilding and Engineering Unions; and though the constituent unions retained their right to independent action, the Confederation took over the conduct of general wage negotiations which covered all the grades of workers employed in this group.

The period between the two wars was one of rapidly changing fortune for the engineering industry. The prosperity brought by the first war came to an abrupt end in 1920 with the onset of the depression, and the industry as a whole did not recover until the rearmament programme which heralded the second World War was set on foot in the late 'thirties. But whilst certain sections of the industry suffered profound dislocation and chronic unemployment, others, such as those making aircraft, motor-cars, electrical equipment and a wide range of consumption goods, expanded very greatly. The electrical engineering section, which had employed just over 5% of the workers covered by the engineering group in 1907, accounted for 15·4% in 1924 and for 22·5% in 1935. Similarly those employed in motor, cycle and aircraft manufacture represented 7·4% of the total in 1907 and 20·4% in 1924 but by 1935 they accounted for 28·5% of the group.[1]

Not only had the relative balance of trades altered but there had been a remarkable change in methods and materials. Special types of steel and a long list of non-ferrous metals and alloys now came to play a big part in production; and belt assembly, where the output was sufficiently large to justify it, took the place of skilled bench fitting. The result of all these changes was that apprenticeship ceased, even in theory, to be the main method of entry into these industries. The Enquiry into Apprenticeship conducted by the Ministry of Labour in 1926 showed that of all workers under 21 in the industry, only 32% were apprentices, and a further 11% learners, and only three-fifths of firms trained any apprentices at all. There was no general scheme for apprenticeship which covered the industry as a whole though the National Federation of Engineering and Allied Employers issued a form for the use of those members who wished to have it; and the agreements varied from locality to locality. The industry was so widely distributed and contained such a great variety of size and type of firm that it was difficult to

[1] Censuses of Production, 1924 and 1935.

make any generalizations that would be widely applicable; but for the most part apprentices were sons of the adult workers employed by the firms and served for a period of five years at wages which began at about 10s. 6d. a week in the first year and ended in the last at 25s. 8d. After this the young man usually served as an improver for a period which might be anything from six months to two years, on conditions and at wage rates agreed by the local union, which usually meant that the rate was 10s. less than that earned by the fully qualified man.

In some cases apprenticeship was taken very seriously—about thirty firms had well organized works schools—but, for the most part, boys picked up what knowledge they could by watching others at work. During the first year or two there was a good deal of wasted time as wages were so low that there was little incentive to economize the boys' labour or to make sure that they were making good use of their opportunities to learn. A great many spent most of their time fetching and carrying, sweeping up and making tea.

The ratio of apprentices to journeymen, which had been such a burning question earlier on, had ceased to be considered so urgent when the Union expanded to include all grades within its ranks, and by an agreement made in 1937 the right of the Union to negotiate on behalf of apprentices was specifically conceded. It was then agreed that the wages of 'junior male workers' should fluctuate on a national basis in a fixed proportion to those of adults, and though this agreement was designed primarily for those not undergoing training, the employers agreed that apprentices should not be placed in a less favourable position in this respect than that of other young workers. But whilst the Union's national policy no longer concerned itself with the regulation of entry, many localities enforced their own ratios on the firms within the area, with the result that there was a great diversity in practice between regions and between different branches of the industry. In some sections the permitted proportion of apprentices to adults was as little as 1 to 10; in others, notably the instrument makers, two-thirds of all those employed were apprentices or learners.

The outbreak of the second World War threw an even greater strain on the engineering and shipbuilding industries than had the first. There were 1,600,000 employed in them in 1939,[1] but when employment in them had reached its peak in 1943–4, there were three and a quarter million. More than a million of these were semi-skilled women, many of whom would withdraw almost as soon as hostilities were ended, and the total numbers in the industry had already been reduced by 300,000 by 1946. But the industry had an immense amount of civilian backlog in production to make good and a total labour force of 1,850,000 in 1948 had grown to 2,118,000 by 1950.[2]

It is obvious that this enormous increase could not have been possible if apprenticeship had been required for any large proportion of workers, and in fact, already in 1940, agreements were made to allow the introduction of semi-skilled men to do jobs hitherto reserved for skilled workers provided that a register of such 'dilutees' was maintained and an undertaking given by the employers to replace them by skilled labour as soon as it became once more available. The continued post-war expansion of these industries has retained these clauses in the agreements covering employment, and there are a very large number of men now engaged on jobs rated as skilled who have been upgraded from other work.

In addition to these there are probably many—though how many it is impossible to estimate—who have upgraded themselves. Despite the high degree of trade union organization in these industries there are large numbers of men, particularly those working in small firms, whose union membership is merely formal. They pay their dues and demand union rates but take little further interest in policy or rules. If a man is taken on by the firm to do a job and seems able to do it sufficiently well not to be a nuisance to his workmates,

---

[1] Ministry of Labour and National Service, Report for 1939–46, Cmd. 7225.
[2] These figures are not quite comparable with the earlier ones as the records are taken from those insured against unemployment, and this includes a rather wider range since 1946, when unemployment insurance was extended to cover all employees, manual and non-manual, whatever their pay. But the number of non-manual persons thus insured for the first time is not a very high proportion of the total. Annual Abstract of Statistics, 1956.

they do not bother to go into his past and find out if he has a 'right' to be so employed. With the present shortage of labour he is unlikely to come in as a blackleg so no fears are aroused and once he has held down such a job his insurance card becomes evidence that he is to be included in that category of skilled worker for the future.

Meanwhile, however, following the consultation with regard to the future recruitment to skilled industries, of which mention has already been made, a memorandum of agreement between the Engineering and Allied Employers' National Federation and the Manual Workers' Unions affiliated to the Confederation of Shipbuilding and Engineering Unions was drawn up and published in 1947 under the title *Recruitment and Training of Juveniles for the Engineering Industry*. The main terms of this memorandum are:

(1) The establishment of a National Joint Body consisting of representatives of the Engineering and Allied Employers' National Federation and the Confederation of Shipbuilding and Engineering Unions to agree general conditions of recruitment and training. In addition, the establishment of Local Training Committees consisting of local representatives of Employers' Associations and the Union to co-operate with the Youth Employment Service to recruit suitable boys and safeguard the maintenance of agreed conditions of training. These bodies are concerned only with recruitment and training and not with wages which remain the function of the existing machinery.

(2) The National Joint Body has the duty of laying down minimum standards relating to the employment and training of young workers, and of ensuring compliance through the existing industrial machinery. Whilst young people are not prevented from entering the employment of their choice, they shall as far as practicable be diverted from employment which does not comply with the agreed standards.

(3) The National Joint Body must try to secure agreement upon the conditions of apprenticeship training throughout the various crafts of the industries.

(4) All apprentices shall be engaged upon written agreement.

(5) Arrangements shall be made for the systematic release of apprentices during normal working hours for attendance at educational courses as follows:

(*a*) Until County Colleges are set up employers are recommended to allow apprentices up to the age of 18 one day a week (or its equivalent) to attend courses at technical or other schools, and to pay them the time rate of wage.

(*b*) When County Colleges are set up attendance of apprentices will be controlled by statutory requirements. For those over 18 attendance of apprentices is a concession to be made in the case of those who show such aptitude and progress as to justify it.

(*c*) Voluntary attendance at evening classes should be encouraged but not made a condition of apprenticeship.

(*d*) Arrangements shall be made as far as is practicable for an apprentice to receive some training in trades closely related to the one he is learning.

(*e*) As far as possible arrangements shall be made to exchange apprentices between works in order to widen their experience.

(6) Craft Apprenticeship begins at 16 and ends at 21. Although a general reduction of the five-year period is not approved, Local Training Committees shall give consideration to special cases, e.g. where a boy has satisfactorily followed a full-time course of suitable standard before beginning his apprenticeship, but in no case shall apprenticeship end before the age of 21.

(7) The National Joint Body and Local Committees shall also give attention to the selection and training of young workers who are not apprenticed, with a view to making them more adaptable and better qualified for advancement in the industry.

The trades which are recognized as those for which apprenticeship is required are:

Engineering

Armature Winders	Capstan Setters
Blacksmiths	Coppersmiths

Engineering—continued

Coremakers	Pipe Fitters
Draughtsmen	Platers
Electrical Testers	Press Tool Setters
Electricians and Wiremen	Roll Turners
Fitters	Sheet Metal and Panel Beaters
Instrument Makers	Template Makers
Machine Tool Setters	Toolmakers
Machinists	Tool Room Craftsmen
Millwrights	Turners
Moulders	Welders
Pattern-makers	

Shipbuilding

Acetylene Burners	Loftsmen
Boatbuilders	Millwrights
Boilermakers	Patternmakers
Caulkers	Platers
Drillers	Plumbers
Electricians	Riggers
Fitters	Riveters
Holders On	Rivet Heaters
Joiners	Shipwrights
Ironfounders	Turners
Ironmoulders	Welders

It is interesting to note in the terms of the Memorandum of Agreement that there is no mention of the matter which was earlier the main subject of controversy with regard to apprenticeship, i.e. the ratio of apprentices to journeymen. With the unprecedented expansion of this group of industries the constant problem has been to attract enough workers to meet the continually growing demands rather than to restrict entry. But though there is no national agreement on this matter the Unions still keep a wary eye on the dangers of training too many workers for jobs which command high rates of pay. It is recognized that there may be a local surplus even when there is an overall national shortage, and the local branches of the Union are empowered to negotiate and enforce local ratios whenever they consider the situation demands it.

This wariness for the future is particularly apparent in

the shipbuilding industry which is the only one of this group which nowadays maintains a strict watch over ratios. Ship-building is still extremely highly skilled because it does not permit of the breakdown of separate operations into semi-skilled processes to anything like the extent that is possible in general engineering. Each ship is built to the specifications of the persons commissioning it, and except in time of war, it is rare to build any large number to a standard pattern. The years between the wars were disastrous in this industry, which was one of those with the highest and most con-tinuous rates of unemployment; the percentage of unemploy-ment never fell below 21% during the period from 1924–38 and at one time rose as high as 62%. In some districts as many as two-thirds of the men ostensibly attached to the industry were out of work for years at a time. This experience has left a deep scar on the minds of the workers, and their unions are so terrified that they might once again find them-selves in this position that they are determined to do all in their power to prevent it by restricting entry to the trades to the numbers they think likely to get employment if a reces-sion occurs. It is significant that there is much greater insist-ence on the maintenance of ratios with regard to the crafts that are peculiar to shipbuilding than there is in those which are common to several types of production. Amongst joiners and engineers, for example, there are a large number of other fields of employment if shipbuilding declines; for ship-wrights and welders shipbuilding is the only possible outlet, and the unions are much more concerned about entry to the latter crafts than they are to the former. The National Agreement does not mention any ratio for these crafts but the unions maintain a strict proportion—in some areas 1 : 3, in others 1 : 5.

There does not seem to be any disagreement on general principles in this matter between the employers and the unions, for the employers recognize that in a highly fluc-tuating industry there is some sense in adjusting numbers to long-term demands. Difficulties arise however when the re-gional union restricts calculation of the permitted ratio to the individual firm rather than to the industry of the area, for this cuts down the number of qualified workers by the chance of whether all firms are prepared to undertake training or not. As however (as will be shown later) it is rare for shipbuilding firms to be without apprentices this danger is not as great as might be feared. A more serious problem arises as a result of changing techniques. The most revolutionary change in shipbuilding methods is the rapid substitution of welding for riveting. The changeover has taken place so rapidly that the number of boys willing to become apprenticed to riveting has shown a sharp decline, for it is looked upon as a dying trade, whilst at the same time the Boiler Makers' Society continues to maintain a rigorous ratio of 1 : 5 amongst welders. As the number of adult welders in existence was, of course, geared to the older methods of production expansion has been severely restricted, with the result that this has become one of the most serious bottlenecks in the industry.

The agreed Memorandum was not intended as a blueprint to be followed in every detail by every firm. On the contrary, its aim was to ensure the adoption of certain minimum standards which would be maintained through general supervision. Many of the big engineering firms already had excellent training schemes which it was realized were far above any standard that could be imposed on the industry as a whole, and the purpose of the agreed scheme was to put a firm foundation under the establishments that had not developed good schemes of their own, rather than to try to introduce a uniform pattern.

Having issued the Memorandum, what happened? At the national level no further action was taken to determine how far the scheme was implemented. The National Joint Body and the Local Committees were duly set up and it was hoped that all would be well, but at the time this enquiry was undertaken nothing had been done by the sponsoring bodies. A first survey was being planned but had not yet begun to be made. It may be that it is this lack of any central encouragement which accounts for the very patchy situation disclosed by this enquiry.

All the sections of the industry contain a great diversity of firms as regards size, for even shipbuilding, surprisingly enough, has a large number of small firms, most of which are primarily concerned with boatbuilding. But whilst in each case the majority of establishments employ under 100 workers by far the largest proportion of workers are employed by the smaller number of bigger firms. In general engineering, for example, whilst 88% of the establishments employ under 100 and 9% between 100 and 500, $52\frac{1}{2}$% of the workers work in firms which have over 500 workers and 20% in firms employing over 2,000.

In electrical engineering the distinction is even more marked, for whereas $83\frac{1}{2}$% are establishments with less than 100 workers, and $15\frac{1}{2}$% those with between 100 and 500, 72% of the employees are in establishments employing over 500, and $58\frac{1}{2}$% in those with over 1,000 workers. In iron foundries 73·7% are employed in firms with over 100, though these represent little more than a quarter of the establish-ments, and in iron and steel manufacture more than two-thirds are in establishments which each have over 1,000 workers.

In assessing the results of the enquiry account must be taken of the fact that the replies received did not come in equal proportions from all size groups. In mechanical engineering the discrepancy is slight, for replies were received from 58 to 60% in each case, but in electrical engineering, on the other hand, whereas between 60 and 65% of all groups employing from 100 to 5,000 returned answers, less than one quarter of the small firms—those employing less than 100—provided information, and the experience of this group is therefore inadequately represented in the results. As however this group employs only 10·7% of the total number engaged in the industry this is perhaps not a very serious lack. In the iron and steel sections 100% replies were returned from the largest firms—those employing 1,000 and over, 85% from those with 500–1,000, $66\frac{1}{2}$% from those with 100–500 but only 43% from those with smaller units. Here again this is not very important, as only 4% of the labour force is employed in this last group of firms. In the ship-building industry it is the boatbuilders who are inadequately represented in the returns, for whereas three-quarters of the establishments employing over 1,000 sent replies, the response of the other sections was less adequate and varied from 39% to 48%. This deficiency is more serious in that about 40% of the labour force is employed in the establishments with under 1,000 workers, nearly 15% of them in the middle size of firm, that is, between 500 and 1,000 from which the lowest proportion of replies—39%—was received. On the whole, therefore, with the exception of the boatbuilding category, the replies should give a fair indication of the situation. From the iron foundries the answers represented 68% of the firms with over 100 employees and this section covers nearly 90% of the total number employed.

There is a further bias to be noted in the firms included in the enquiry. The names of those to whom the questionnaires were sent were obtained from the membership lists of employers' associations. These firms were classified according to geographical location and number of employees, and a random sample taken, as explained in Chapter III. This means that the firms which are not affiliated to their respective associations are not represented in the sample, and it is impossible to say how far their experience differs from that of those who are members. These various bodies do however include within their membership by far the majority of firms within their scope.

In the middle of the year in which the enquiry was made (1956) the unfilled vacancies notified to the Ministry of Labour and National Service in the engineering industry totalled 30,000—22,000 of them in mechanical and 8,000 of them in electrical engineering—and a further 6,000 in metal manufacture. Of these a very large proportion were in skilled crafts and the shortage was evidently fairly general because almost all the firms in the enquiry spoke of shortages of skilled men. Of the mechanical engineering firms one-seventh of the smallest firms (below 100) reported they had no difficulty in getting skilled workers, but almost all others had shortages, which were particularly serious in the case of fitters, turners and toolmakers. These three trades were mentioned most often by all sizes of firm from the smallest to the largest. This being so it is sur-

prising to find how large a number of firms had no apprentices at all on their books. Just about half of the
firms with less than 100 workers (and this group between
them employ 19% of the total) were in this position. Only
three of these firms did not employ skilled workers and presumably the rest depend on other firms to train their
workers for them. Apprenticeship problems must evidently
be a function of size, for about one-fifth of the firms with
100–500 workers were without apprentices whilst all the
firms larger than this had considerable numbers, and thi
means that the larger firms have the responsibility of training
enough skilled men not only for themselves but for a very
large number of firms of smaller size. As has been mentioned
the small firms (below 100 employees) in the electrical engineering section are inadequately represented in the sample
and in any case this category employs only a very small proportion of the total labour force. Yet it is worth noting that
only one of the firms in this group making a return had any
apprentices at all. Here however, unlike the mechanical
engineering group there is a similar situation amongst the
largest firms. More than half the firms with 100–500 employees had no apprentices and a considerable number of
the largest firms were in the same position even in the group
with employees numbering up to 5,000. Here again, turners
and toolmakers were generally in short supply though certain of the largest firms reported adequate staffing. In shipbuilding only two very small firms were without apprentices,
the majority employing very considerable numbers of them
(two firms had over 500 each, though in each of these cases
there were over 5,000 employees;) yet even so most firms
noted a shortage of skilled workers, particularly amongst
riveters and platers.

Amongst iron and steel firms more than half of those with
less than 500 employees (responsible for 21% of the total
number employed) had no apprentices, though all employed
skilled workers and most reported shortages of various kinds.
The same situation obtains in iron foundries but to an
even greater extent. Of the smaller firms employing over
one-fifth (22%) of the total personnel, two-thirds have no

apprentices and, surprising here, one very large firm (with over 3,000 employees) was also entirely without apprentices whilst certain others had only a very few. Yet the shortage of moulders in particular seems to be acute, and that of pattern makers and coremakers only a little less so.

The general impression gained from this Survey seems to be that the burden of training future supplies of skilled workers is very unevenly spread throughout the industry. On the whole, in all sections the smaller establishments do not take their share, though almost all employ adult skilled men, and this means that these firms draw off the trained men from others that are fulfilling their responsibilities under the agreed scheme. In some cases the problem lies not with the willingness of the firm to train but of the boy to apply. General and electrical engineering do not, as a whole, experience any great difficulty in attracting young workers, and the large and well-known firms particularly can pick and choose from an extensive waiting list; though even amongst these sections it is not always easy for the smaller firm to get the workers it would be willing to train. The situation is entirely different in iron foundries, where practically every firm replying to the questionnaire spoke of the difficulty of attracting apprentices. In discussion on this point several said that even offers of considerably higher pay than that earned by apprentices in other crafts failed to get over the difficulty. Often enough it was not the boy himself who objected to entering the 'dirty craft' but his parents who withdrew him after a trial period had shown what this trade involved in dirt and wear and tear on clothes. The position here seems to be extremely serious, for one firm after another expressed the view that the present number of boys training was far below their long-term needs. This dislike of dirty jobs shows itself also in certain sections of shipbuilding. The shortage of skilled men is widely spread as a result of the operation of the ratio principle, but it is particularly acute amongst platers, plumbers and boilersmiths, for which crafts many of the firms find it difficult to get boys to apply, or to remain once they have had some experience of the work.

The principle followed by most firms is to take on boys at

the age of 15 when they first leave school, so as to provide an opportunity both for the boy and for the employer to decide whether an apprenticeship is advisable. During this time the boy gets to know the layout of the shops, the main processes, the names of the tools and the chief types of work produced. In some firms, particularly those with well-organized works schools, care is taken at the outset through induction courses to give the young recruit some insight into the new and bewildering world he is entering for the first time; but this is still fairly exceptional and for the most part he is left to try to find out for himself by his own observation or by the answers he gets to the questions he puts to his seniors. At the end of his first year he decides—or the firm decides for him with his agreement—to which craft he shall be attached, and after that point he begins to specialize. There are some firms in which apprentices to several crafts learn together for the first year of their training and do not make the final decision which is going to dominate the rest of their lives until they have seen a little of the actual work done by them, but more usually this important step is taken as soon as the apprenticeship begins and it is almost impossible later to change from one to another. The preliminary year from 15 to 16 serves a double purpose. Not only does it give the boy a chance to learn his way about, but in view of the fact that there is no special form of selection, it is the only way to eliminate the certain misfits. Firms with a very high reputation usually have more applications for apprenticeship vacancies than they can accommodate and those with good training schemes take a fair amount of trouble to select on the basis of school records and interviews. But the majority seem to be very much more casual in their methods and trust to their belief that any boy who is obviously unsuitable will be picked out during the first year and that the remainder can learn one craft just as well as another. It seems to be rare for any attempt at more serious vocational guidance to be undertaken.

A number of firms, including some of the largest, recruit all their apprentices through the Youth Employment Service, and it may be supposed that the officers have at least attempted some rough and ready selection on the basis of aptitudes; but as far as the firms in this enquiry are concerned, as many do not make use of the Youth Employment Service, or do so only to get additional boys if those making direct application prove insufficient.

Considering the somewhat haphazard methods of selection it is surprising to find how rare it is for the apprenticeship to be cancelled before it is completed. Questions were specifically asked on this point and very few firms had any cancellations to report. One of the largest firms, employing 6,000 workers, said that there might possibly have been two or three during the last five years but certainly not more than this, and this seems to be the general experience. Having once undertaken to train, most apprentices continue for the full term of five years. This is certainly greatly influenced by the fact that the Ministry of Labour allows deferment from National Service to any apprentice undergoing a recognized training until he has finished it at the age of 21, and the vast majority of apprentices take advantage of this privilege.

When the Memorandum on Training was agreed, a carefully graded system was drawn up in respect of each craft, showing what the apprentice should be taught during each period of his five years. This had naturally to be done in fairly general terms, for it was realized that the type of training provided must depend on the nature of the work done by the firm; but emphasis was put on the importance of ensuring that the boy gets an all-round experience that will fit him to undertake any job that falls within the scope of his craft. The theoretical basis of this work would, it was assumed, be taught the apprentice during his days at the technical college (or County College when established) where he would also be able to undertake some practical work, but his main practical experience, it was assumed, would necessarily be gained by doing the various jobs himself in the works. The scheme was silent however on the way in which this practical training was to be gained; and in fact this is done mainly in the way in which apprentices have gained their experience through hundreds of years, that is, by watching an older man at work. In theory the youth is under the supervision of the older man whose task it is to pass on his skill and knowledge and answer the questions of his junior. What, in fact, does this instruction amount to?

This is a question to which it is not possible to give a definite answer because there are so many different interpretations of 'teaching' and 'supervision'. There are many firms with excellently worked-out training schemes lavishly illustrated in brochures of which the firms are justly proud. These publications show an intending recruit and his parents exactly what he can expect to learn during each three–six months of his training, but who is to *teach* him these things is another matter. At a Conference attended by those responsible for craft training in over 100 of the largest engineering firms in the country and including those with the most carefully worked-out schemes for training, it was rather ruefully agreed that, on the whole, the administrative set-up was much more carefully designed than the actual training given. In these firms, all of which have a high sense of responsibility to their young workers, great care has been given to the time that should be devoted to each branch of the craft so as to make certain that the boy is given an all-round training. The Apprentice Master constantly reviews the apprentice's work so as to ensure that he does not get stuck in any one department because he is proving useful there, but that his needs as trainee should take precedence over his productive value. 'But,' as the Director of Training in one of the largest firms employing many thousands of workers admitted, 'the real trouble is that there is nobody to show him how to do the job. We have worked out a carefully graded scheme of training but what we have not done is to provide somebody to say "No, George, don't do it that way, *this* is the right way to use the tool", and we have to be honest enough to admit that, however excellently worked-out on paper our schemes may be, this is where we fall down. We have excellent administrative supervision but there is little practical teaching.' After some hesitation at hearing such frank speaking, the others agreed that this was indeed a true picture.

In theory a boy is attached to a skilled worker who is

supposed to show him how to do a job and correct him when he tries his own hand at it. But these skilled workers do not volunteer for this work; the foreman in charge of that section apportions the apprentices as he thinks fit—sometimes no doubt with an attempt at rough justice—in saddling men in turn with the responsibility, and sometimes, perhaps, choosing those that have proved complaisant in the past. Most craftsmen are anxious to get on with their own work and rather impatient of giving explanations or, perhaps, find difficulty in expressing themselves. Where they are paid piece rates their teaching may involve them in a considerable loss if the trainee is not very quick in the uptake. At the Conference mentioned above one Training Officer said that his firm paid a sum of 7s. 6d. a week as compensation, but at the piece rates then ruling (1956) this would allow of very little time to be taken off one's work to supervise the apprentice, without considerable financial sacrifice.

At the same time the old complaint that so much of a boy's time was wasted in non-productive work is no longer justified; for the wages paid (in conjunction with the cost of releasing the boy for one day a week) are sufficient to ensure that care is taken to make him valuable as quickly as possible. Payment varies with age and is agreed as a proportion of the wage of the skilled adult as follows:—

Age of apprentice	Proportion of Adult rate
16 years	$27\frac{1}{2}\%$
17 ,,	$32\frac{1}{2}\%$
18 ,,	45%
19 ,,	$52\frac{1}{2}\%$
20 ,,	$62\frac{1}{2}\%$

Higher rates are specified for foundry apprentices and for pattern-making apprentices.

BUILDING

Although the Building Industry has been very much influenced by increased mechanization and by the introduction of new materials and methods, there remains greater scope for the craftsman in it than in any other major industry.

This is due both to the nature of building and to the structure of the industry. Doors and windows can be prefabricated ready for fitting, but the building itself must be erected on the site. It is therefore impossible to use mass production methods, and the use of machinery has been of more influence in lightening the work of the unskilled labourer than in altering the job of the skilled man. Machinery, other than rather simple types, is not economic even for this purpose except on comparatively large projects and, as a very large part of the industry is engaged in the construction of single houses or workshops, most of the work must continue to be done by traditional methods. Moreover a considerable proportion of all building labour is engaged on maintenance work or the adaptation of existing premises to other uses, and these by their nature are jobs that do not lend themselves to any degree of standardization. The Ministry of Works estimated in 1948 that 38% of the total output of the industry was maintenance work whilst another 11% was accounted for by civil engineering works and their maintenance. A census of operatives taken in the following year showed that just under 40% of the workers were employed on ordinary repairs and maintenance, plus 13% on war damage and conversion of houses, leaving under 48% on new constructional work of all types.

The wide range of building operations from a minor repair to a roof or door at one limit, to the construction of a huge factory or the building of a complete new town at the other, allows of the existence of a greater diversity of types of firm than is found in most other occupations, spreading from the one-man business at one extreme to the large concern employing over 5,000 operatives at the other. Of the firms in the industry in 1948 42% were one-man businesses and 36% employed no more than five persons.

Usually the smaller the firm the more it concentrates on repair and maintenance work, and the larger it is the greater the emphasis on new construction. In the largest firms, for example, 88% of the work is construction, whereas in those with under 5 operatives (and this group employs 11% of all operatives) it is only $13\frac{1}{2}$%; and in those slightly larger (6–19

workers)—accounting for nearly 20% of the labour force it is
$28\frac{1}{2}\%$. In the medium-sized firms (those with less than 500
workers) the proportions of new work and maintenance are
just about equal.[1]

As a result of the varying emphasis of types of work
amongst firms of different sizes the distribution of craftsmen is not spread evenly throughout the industry. Amongst
the smaller firms (those with 1–5 operatives) nearly 80% are
craftsmen, and there is very nearly the same proportion
among firms with 6–19 workers; whereas the largest firms
employ $73\frac{1}{2}\%$ labourers and only $26\frac{1}{2}\%$ skilled men. In
addition at the time of the census, there were reckoned to
be about 50,000 working builders who employ no workers at
all, and who probably have graduated to this position after
working for a time for some other firm. (This number is
now reduced to about 38,000.[2]) This lopsided distribution of
craftsmen is particularly important in view of the problems
(discussed later) which confront the small firm in taking and
training apprentices.

Building firms in this country fall into a number of well-
defined categories and though there is no rigid line of demarcation between them they tend to operate mainly within
certain fields:

(1) A few very large firms capable of dealing with the
biggest jobs of any kind in any part of the country or abroad.

(2) A much larger number of medium-sized firms able
to undertake big jobs of most types but which usually confine their operations to one locality.

(3) The speculative builders who devote themselves primarily to developing housing estates to their own design
and who often sub-contract with (6) (see below) for certain
types of labour.

(4) A large number of general purpose builders whose
main work consists of repairs and alterations to existing
buildings but who also often erect small groups of houses or
a single cottage.

---

[1] Report of the Working Party on the Building Industry, 1950, pp. 5–6.
[2] *The Review of Productivity in the Building Industry*, The British Productivity
Council, p. 6.

(5) A very large number of jobbing builders occupied almost exclusively with repair work.

(6) 'Labour only' firms who supply operatives for certain operations as sub-contractors to larger firms. This class of firm has increased greatly since the war, especially on housing schemes. Owing to the difficulty of recruiting adequate supplies of labour the firm contracting for a large building or estate sub-contracts to other firms for specialist jobs, i.e. it arranges to have the bricklaying done by a firm which does nothing else, and the plastering similarly done by another specialist firm. A sub-contracting firm can often offer higher wages and more regular employment than a general builder. Since the end of the war, for example, bricklayers have agreed to the introduction of piece rates, and a specialist firm can step up output by paying in this way; but a general builder, many of whose men are on maintenance work which, of course, does not lend itself to anything but time rates, cannot pay a section of his bricklayers piece rates because they are on construction work, without causing general unrest within the firm.

This structure leads to serious obstacles to any training programme. Repair and maintenance work is essentially 'jobbing' in character, as is also true of the 'one house at a time' type of new construction work. Small firms, i.e. those with less than 20 employees who undertake this work (and between them they employ 30·4% of the labour force) lead a fairly hand-to-mouth existence, not from the point of view of financial stability but from that of long-term planning of their work. They are therefore often unwilling to bind themselves to take apprentices for whom they must be responsible for five years. In the post-war period with its constant acute shortage of manpower a large number of these firms have kept men on the books between jobs so as to escape the risk that they might not be able to lure them back if they were once allowed to go. But the memories of the past, when often there were considerable gaps between jobs, make them afraid to take on boys for as long as five years with the obligation to pay them whether they find work for them to do or not. The very large firms on the other hand often take on local labour supplies in the place where the buildings are to be constructed, and as far as their permanent workers are concerned, can employ only those who are able to be mobile. Here the adolescent worker is a drag. Such a firm cannot provide progressive training for apprentices who 'stay put' unless it is also willing to undertake the burdensome work of housing and supervising a group of young people away from their own homes. In addition, the growth of the 'labour only' firm reduces still further the number of employers with the facilities and willingness to train young recruits to the industry.

It is not only the jobbing character of so much building work which makes training difficult but also the fact that, as an outdoor occupation, it necessarily suffers from interruptions due to weather. Building operations must stop during heavy rain or snow or fog, and largely on this account the industry used to be highly seasonal. Building workers used to calculate that they might have to face 6–8 weeks without work during the year, and employers have hesitated to bind themselves to an apprentice whose wages they would have to pay wet or fine. This source of interruptions to work is constant, but building has also suffered from severe cyclical depression. When trade in general is slack, industrial firms postpone the building of extensions or the establishment of new branches, and this means that building has always been one of the first industries to show the signs of a downward curve in economic prosperity. Just prior to the war, 18% of the labour force belonging to the industry was registered as unemployed, and in the depressed areas, such as South Wales and the north of England, where the decline in the export industries reduced the demand both for factories and houses, one in three of all building employees was out of a job.

Since the war unemployment has been practically non-existent except when shortage of raw materials has held up work, but the high rate of unemployment usual before the war, and the insecurity that was the characteristic of employment even during times of prosperity, made employers unwilling to take on apprentices, and boys unwilling to offer themselves for training. In the Report of an Enquiry into

Apprenticeship and Training for Skilled Trades published in 1928 it was calculated that only 36% of building employers had any apprentices at all.

This situation was made much worse by the exigencies of war. House building was one of the earliest war casualties, for all available men and materials had to be switched to war production. All less essential building stopped completely and this meant that there ceased to be any projects available on which workers could be trained in any of the finer crafts. The construction needed was the erection of munition factories or the making of airfields with their equipment, and none of this gave much chance to the man skilled in the highest grades of workmanship such as would be required in the building of a fine theatre or a large country house. Moreover the siting of new building was determined primarily on strategic grounds, where it was hoped that essential war production could be carried on with less disturbance from air raids, and such sites were usually too far from established centres of population to provide openings for young workers. All this meant that opportunities for apprenticeship were still further drastically reduced. The effect of this can be seen in the returns made at the request of the Ministry of Works in 1944 by just under 40,000 builders, all of whom had declared that they had previously employed apprentices. In the seven chief building crafts—carpenter and joiner; bricklayer; plumber; painter; plasterer; mason; slater—there had been in 1939 a total of 71,410 apprentices under training. In September, 1944, there were under 49,191.[1]

Apprehension about the future led the Government to take action early in the war by the appointment of a committee to consider Training for the Building Industry, which issued its Report in February, 1943.[2]

It was recognized that after the war there would be need for a much larger building industry in order to make up the backlog of construction that had been held up during the war years, as well as to replace and repair bomb-damaged buildings. Without an adequate labour force reconstruction

[1] B.A.T.C., 2nd Report, 1945, Appendix IIc, p. 35.
[2] Cmd. 6428.

would be impossible. The Committee calculated that an annual intake of between 15,000 and 20,000 apprentices would be needed simply to make good normal wastage by death, age, and illness, without any addition to the depleted labour force. In view of the recruitment in the past it was unlikely that this would be achieved unless there were some authoritative body to encourage and supervise it, and the Report recommended that a new body to be called the Building Apprenticeship and Training Council representative of the industry should be set up. The functions proposed for the Council were:

(*a*) A comprehensive review of existing apprenticeship schemes.

(*b*) The definition of minimum standards to which apprenticeship schemes should conform.

(*c*) The maintenance of a register of apprentices serving under apprenticeship schemes and the issue of certificates on completion of training.

(*d*) The promotion of publicity designed to stimulate interest in building as a career.

(*e*) Practical methods of encouraging employers and apprentices to participate in approved schemes.

The Council was set up immediately after the publication of the Report and began its work at once. It consisted of representatives of all the relevant associations of employers and operatives, of the professional institutions and educational bodies and of the related government departments; and the Ministry of Works became responsible for financing the Council and providing the secretariat. The Council continued under the Government's aegis until 1955 when it was felt that foundations for future developments had been firmly laid, and its functions were transferred to the National Joint Council for the Building Industry. From that date the industry alone became responsible for it. As the Chairman of the B.A.T.C., Sir F. W. Legget, said in relinquishing his office, 'they laid down their task confident in the knowledge that their apprenticeship and training have been established on a firm foundation and that the work that they attempted to do in reviving apprenticeship schemes and observing on matters of recruitment, education and training will be continued by the Building Industry'.[1]

For the Government to take the initiative in attempting to stimulate the supply and supervise the training of skilled manpower of an industry was a new experiment, and building remains the one field of employment in which such assistance has been given. It threw all its influence on the side of the organization and development of good schemes of apprenticeship.

'The Government fully endorses the view', says Command Paper 6428, 1943, 'that in the Building Industry a high value attaches to the apprenticeship system as the recognized method of training for employment and of entry into the ranks of skilled workers. The industry has not in the past neglected the importance of developing its apprenticeship schemes, but it is generally recognized that they follow no comprehensive and systematic plan and that the time has come to survey the whole field with a view to putting recruitment and apprenticeship training on the soundest possible basis and maintaining such bases at all times. A first objective was to secure that no person should enter the industry as a skilled worker unless he had been properly trained. The "back-door" to the industry must be closed.'

One valuable consequence of this Government contact is that we have more knowledge of the demand for and the supply of skilled workers in building than in any other industry, for one of the first tasks of the B.A.T.C. was to estimate the probable needs of the industry for manpower after the war and to keep this estimate under constant review in the light of changing economic circumstances. When the White Paper was issued in 1943 it was estimated that a building labour force of one and a quarter million, of whom 625,000 would be skilled craftsmen, would be required annually if this number of skilled workers was to be reached and maintained. Almost immediately after the end of the war, however, it was realized that the estimate of the rate of reconstruction had been much too optimistic. The continued shortage of

[1] B.A.T.C. Final Report, July, 1956.

raw materials held back rebuilding; but even more, the frequent sterling crises reduced the rate of capital investment. The demand for steel and timber had to be reduced for all kinds of building, and as the construction that *was* allowed was concentrated on large projects and local authority housing estates (in which as was shown above the proportion of craftsmen to labourers is smaller), the number of skilled men required was further reduced, so that an annual intake of 22,000 apprentices instead of the 25,000 first envisaged became the Council's aim.

Boys are apprenticed however not to the building industry as a whole but to a particular building craft, and the Council thought it useful to consider how many of this 22,000 should be encouraged to attach themselves to each particular type of work. They realized that this was a difficult task because the proportions depend on the kind of building under construction, but they still felt it would be useful to have an indication of what they needed, and they gave the following targets:

Trade	% of industry	Number
Carpenters and Joiners	26	5,700
Painters	25	5,500
Bricklayers	21	4,600
Plumbers	$9\frac{1}{2}$	2,100
Plasterers	8	1,750
Masons	$2\frac{1}{2}$	550
Slaters and Tilers	2	450
Other crafts	6	1,300

It is interesting to see how these estimates of the industry's requirements compare with the actual numbers that were under training in each craft at that time. If the figures of annual intake given above were achieved there would be under training at any one time five times this number in each craft. The target numbers and the actual figures for 1944 are set beside one another for comparison.

Trade	Target	Actual
Carpenters	28,500	19,763
Painters	27,500	7,505

Trade	Target	Actual
Bricklayers	23,000	7,010
Plumbers	10,500	11,948
Plasterers	8,750	1,479
Masons	2,750	723
Slaters	2,250	1,349

It was fairly obvious that some sort of emergency measure had to be taken to bridge the gap between these two sets of figures, and it was for this reason that the B.A.T.C. inaugurated the Apprentice Master Scheme. It was proposed that a contract should be entered into by a Local Authority with a contractor who should become the Apprentice Master, and in order to encourage Local Authorities to do this, both for building new houses and for repairing houses damaged by bombs, the Council agreed to reimburse them for the excess over normal costs in which they would be involved. Where a project under the scheme was to operate on a site remote from a centre of population the Minister of Labour and National Service undertook to provide for the boys a scale of maintenance grants which would subsidize their wages, because the pay of apprentices was insufficient to meet heavy expenses in getting to distant work or in maintaining themselves away from their own homes.

The essentials of the scheme were:

(*a*) That new building projects should be carried out primarily for the training of apprentices and that in particular these projects should include the building and rebuilding of houses.

(*b*) That the proportion of apprentices to craftsmen instructors should be of the order of six or more to one according to the craft and other circumstances of a particular project, and that in specially favourable circumstances the proportion might be as high as twelve to one.

(*c*) That this training should be accepted as conferring full status upon the apprentice and provide for the transfer to an employer as soon as suitable work became available.

(*d*) That the operation of the scheme and supervision of the training should be the responsibility of the Joint Apprenticeship Committee.

91

There proved to be no scarcity of boys willing to be trained in this way, and indeed the number offering themselves was often in excess of the capacity of the scheme to absorb them. So great was the desire to ensure that suitable applicants should not be lost to the industry that certain projects were extended, with consequent increase in the cost over what had been originally anticipated. As a result of this scheme more than 3,000 new houses were built and 7,500 boys received their initial apprenticeship training in 117 areas throughout England and Wales.[1] With the exception of 54 boys all these transferred to the building industry and continued apprenticeship. There are many who believe that the training given by this scheme was in fact sounder than that provided by many private employers, for care was taken to ensure that each boy was given an introduction to general building requirements before selecting the building craft on which he was going to specialize. Moreover the apprentice was given the opportunity to try his hand in the construction of every type of unit even though this slowed up production and increased the eventual cost of the building; and he thus obtained a greater breadth of experience than is always possible in private employment. The scheme remained in existence until 1952 when it was brought to an end as an economy measure.

The Apprentice Master Scheme was designed simply to fill a gap during an exceptional period, but the main work of the B.A.T.C. was to devise a suitable training scheme of a permanent kind. The National Joint Council for the Building Industry, representative of both sides in the industry, had set up a National Joint Apprenticeship Board in the same year that the Council was established to act as a national supervisory body for training within the industry. The Council recommended that regional and local apprenticeship committees representative of employers and operatives in the areas should also be appointed to take charge of the detailed day to day administrative supervision under this national authority, and that to these committees should be entrusted the control of recruitment and the review of facilities provided

[1] B.A.T.C. Final Report, 1956, Appendix 9.

by the Local Authorities or technical instruction for building craft apprentices.

The scheme recommended by the Council had certain features which distinguish it from those already discussed for the engineering and shipbuilding industries. Like those it followed the traditional pattern of requiring a five-year apprenticeship beginning at 16 and ending at 21 with provision for release for one day a week for those under 18 to attend technical instruction; and it also proposed that definite reduction of this period should be allowed to those who had had some previous full-time training. But it differed in two important respects:

(1) It proposed that the apprenticeship agreement, which it was recommended should be in writing, should be signed by four parties—the apprentice, his guardian, the employer, and a representative of the Regional or Local Apprenticeship Committee. The agreement should confer on this fourth party the right to take steps to ensure that the apprentice is instructed in all the branches of his craft. If after enquiry the training was shown to be inadequate the Committee should have the right to cancel the agreement and to transfer the apprentice to another employer.

(2) It laid upon the Council the duty of maintaining a register of apprentices whose agreements conformed to the minimum standards laid down. The purpose of this recommendation was to enable the Regional and Local Apprenticeship Committee as fourth party to the apprenticeship agreement to have full and continuing knowledge of all apprentices under their care.

These recommendations were accepted and the 'Building Industry National Joint Apprenticeship Scheme' was published by the National Joint Council for the Building Industry at the end of 1945. For the first time the conditions covering apprentices became part of the Constitution and Rules of the National Joint Council with the full authority of a national agreement in the same way as wage rates and working conditions. The main provisions of the scheme are as follows:

(1) All boys learning a craft must be bound under a

standard Deed of Apprenticeship provided by the National Joint Council; to this Deed there are four parties—employer, guardian, apprentice and a representative of the appropriate Local or Regional Joint Apprenticeship Committee.

(2) The normal period of apprenticeship is five years which must end not before the 20th nor later than the 21st birthday. In the South this period begins on or after the 15th birthday, but in the Midlands, Northern England, Yorkshire and North-West regions, the approved minimum age is the 16th birthday. This period may be reduced:

(*a*) by one year in the case of a boy who has satisfactorily completed a full pre-apprenticeship course in building at a secondary technical school or other institution, and

(*b*) by two years in the case of a boy who has satisfactorily completed a whole-time Senior Day Course in building of not less than two years' duration provided that the course is approved by the National Joint Apprenticeship Board, and provided also that the period actually served in the trade is not less than three years.

In special circumstances the Regional Joint Apprenticeship Committee may permit a boy to enter into an apprenticeship later than 15 or 16 provided that three full years are served and that the apprenticeship does not end before the 20th or after the 21st birthday.

(3) There is a probationary period of six months beginning at the minimum age for apprenticeship (15 or 16) but this counts as part of the apprenticeship and the Deed is back-dated accordingly.

(4) All apprentices under 18 must attend approved day technical classes (where available) for one day or two half-days a week, and in addition must attend approved evening technical classes on two evenings a week through the period of apprenticeship. The fees both for day and for evening classes must be paid by the employer who must also pay wages in respect of the classes attended during normal working hours.

(5) A Joint Apprenticeship Committee may arrange a

94

transfer to another employer if the original employer is unable to continue the training, or if the committee thinks it in the best interests of the apprentice, but no transfer can take place without the written consent of the Joint Apprenticeship Committee.

(6) When the apprenticeship is satisfactorily completed the Deed is endorsed to that effect both by the employer and by the representative of the Joint Apprenticeship Committee, and it then becomes the property of the apprentice. Upon advice from the Regional Joint Apprenticeship Committee that this has been done an 'Apprentice's Completion Certificate' is issued by the National Joint Apprenticeship Board to the apprentice. He then becomes a fully qualified craftsman entitled to the standard craft rate of pay.

(7) During apprenticeship the apprentice receives wages on a national apprenticeship scale as follows:

Age	Proportion of Craft Rate
15	$\frac{1}{4}$
16	$\frac{1}{3}$
17	$\frac{1}{2}$
18	$\frac{5}{8}$
19	$\frac{3}{4}$
20	$\frac{7}{8}$

It is interesting to note that in this nationally agreed scheme there is no mention of any ratio of apprentices to adults, and it is presumably left to employers to decide how many it is worth their while to train. It is however, accepted that one of the duties of the Local or Regional Joint Apprenticeship Committees is to maintain a constant review of recruitment to the industry and ensure a balanced intake to the constituent crafts. Some committees have found that a ratio of 1 apprentice to 4 craftsmen can be considered a good general guide, but this is by no means universal, and it is extremely rare for any attempt to be made at strict enforcement of this or any other proportion.

The big expansion of the industry during the post-war period and its unprecedented freedom from spells of unemployment probably account for this lack of concern on the part of the trade unions about the possibility of overstimulation of recruitment. As will be shown later it is probable that the unwillingness of many firms to saddle themselves with the responsibility of training young workers does more to keep down the numbers of those capable of offering themselves as fully-trained skilled adults than could be achieved by any firm insistence by the unions on a particular ratio. An apprentice is in no sense cheap labour as at one time he was. On the contrary, in addition to the unusually high proportion of the craftsman's rate that he must be paid, the employer is under contract to pay him wages for one full day on which he is producing nothing, and to meet the cost of his technical education both during day release and throughout the five years that he attends evening classes. Mr. Harvey G. Frost, a leading building employer in East Anglia, and Chairman of the Eastern Counties Regional Joint Apprenticeship Committee, gave it as his opinion (in an interview in 1954) that the apprentice represents on balance a loss to the employer of about £160 for the five years of his apprenticeship.

In the first year after the establishment of the scheme the rate at which boys entered the industry for other than unskilled labouring was said to be in the neighbourhood of 20,000; but in the next year it suffered a severe drop to 13,000.[1] This was probably due to the raising of the school-leaving age from 14–15 in April, 1947, but when the stream of school-leavers was resumed the rate of recruitment still remained far below the desired level. According to reports received by the Ministry of Labour from its local offices this was not due to any serious shortage of applicants but to the lack of vacancies for apprentices. The curtailment of the investment programme, even though this was subsequently partially relaxed, had a serious psychological effect on the industry. Despite a later increase in the volume of work, many feared for the future and were reluctant to commit themselves to a contract covering so long a period as five years. Moreover the restriction of building work to priority projects and to houses of simple standard design put a

[1] B.A.T.C. Special Report on Building Apprentices' Recruitment and Training, 1948.

severe limitation on the scope of apprentice training. It is just the type of firm able to undertake these large schemes in which the proportion of unskilled to skilled labour is particularly large. By the middle of 1949 there were 72,410 boys within the apprenticeship age range who stated they were learning a craft in the building industry (and this obviously includes many not fully apprenticed) whereas if the target figures had been attained there should have been 110,000.[1]

In the middle of 1953 the Ministry of Works took a further census of the manpower position which, while it showed some improvement on the situation, still gave evidence of a serious deficiency in recruitment, particularly in the trowel trades. The intake of apprentices over the whole country and in all crafts was 3·4% of the adult strength as compared with the 4% designated as the required number to replace wastage; but in London, the Midlands and the South-East area (where the competition of other occupations is particularly severe) the intake fell far below this national average. As a result the total number of apprentices in London was only 3·6% of the number of craftsmen, in the South-East area 9·8% and in the Midlands 12·9% in comparison with 27% in Scotland and 20–22% in many other regions.

The different crafts showed a very uneven incidence of shortage, for whereas the apprentice strength of carpenters had reached the target set by B.A.T.C., that of the bricklayers was only 70%; of the painters less than 60% and of plasterers the lowest at 43%.

That many of those classified in the Ministry of Labour statistics as 'learning a craft' are not fully indentured apprentices is corroborated by the comparatively small number registered with the B.A.T.C. The total number of boys registered in the four years after the scheme was inaugurated in 1945 was only 26,590. There was a great variation between regions. In the South-East area, for example, 2,493 of the 3,000 boys learning a craft were registered, whereas in Scotland, of 13,590 there were only 3,358 on the register and in Yorkshire the insignificant number of 860 out of the total number of 7,610. It may be that many of those who were

[1] B.A.T.C. 4th Report, 1949.

unregistered were in fact undergoing training according to the agreed conditions but it is likely that a considerable proportion were 'picking up their skill' rather than being trained, because of the employers' reluctance to bind themselves for so long a time.

There is indeed a long tradition in the building industry of this informal method of entry to skilled work. The Webbs in their *Industrial Democracy* spoke of the London builders at the end of the last century as having ceased entirely to employ boys, and the Operatives' Society of Bricklayers recruited their members from young labourers who were allowed to decide at the age of 25 whether they wished to abandon the hod for the trowel, and were then accepted as skilled workers. The Manchester Slaters' Society admitted to membership any man actually working with a slater, and after serving for seven years in this way he might be recognized as a fully qualified man if his work was of good standard. It is evidently largely through this same system of 'progression' from one grade to another that the depleted ranks of the skilled craftsmen have been filled during the post-war period. The preponderance of the small firm explains the possibility of this method, for the builder with only three or four employees cannot employ specialists for every type of work but expects his few men to turn their hands to whatever is required. The worker thus gets experience of jobs for which he has had no specific training and can move on to another employer on the basis of this experience to specialize in one of the kinds of work he has undertaken in this way. Very few employers bother to enquire whether, or where, a worker has secured full apprenticeship, particularly during the manpower shortage that has characterized the post-war situation. If the man can claim previous experience and can tackle a job with reasonable competence, the employer is content to take him on without too many precise enquiries. This has been made particularly easy because of the large amount of housing estate work undertaken in the last ten or twelve years in which the standardization of simple design has given little scope for really skilled work. It may be that some of the many complaints of poor workmanship heard since a greater variety of building work became possible may be due to the existence of so many men in the industry who are accepted as skilled craftsmen but who have never had the training which would justify their employment as such.

Theoretically it is not permissible for a non-union man to do a craft job and only qualified men are admitted to membership of the unions; but in practice the restriction is not so severe, and the extent to which this infiltration takes place depends to a considerable degree on the strength of the local trade union organization. In many rural and semi-rural areas there are a large number of firms whose workers are not members of unions, or who, even if they are, have no objection to working with others who have not yet become members, so long as there is no shortage of jobs. When these men move on to other areas they get skilled work and if the union is more powerful they join an appropriate organization. Provided they are paid the agreed rate the union does not trouble itself about their early history; and their union membership itself thereafter ensures that they are accepted as fully skilled craftsmen.

The present enquiry covered all sizes of firms and all districts but the proportion of replies received varies greatly from one area to another. So few replies were obtained from Wales and from the North Midlands that these two areas are virtually unrepresented. But the others are reasonably well covered and, fortunately, the areas in which the largest number of firms are situated—London and the South-East, the Midlands, the North-West and Scotland—are particularly well represented, as the proportion of replies received was about two-thirds of those sent. In the East and North regions the proportion was considerably higher. With regard to size, again there is fair representation in the answers received, for from 60–64% of the firms in each category replied. The exceptions are found in two groups—those with 50–100 and those with over 500 employees in which the proportion was round about 50%.

The replies gave clear evidence of the uneven incidence of the burden of training. Three-quarters of the firms with less than 10 employees had no apprentices at all, whereas on the other hand, of the firms employing 100–500 only one-fifth of the firms had no apprentices and some had very large numbers. In the large firms the lack of training facilities is clearly marked. The largest firm in the sample with 24,000 employees of whom 5,525 were skilled, had only 87 apprentices in all the crafts combined; another, with over 13,000 on its pay-roll, including 2,700 skilled craftsmen, had 278 apprentices—a proportion of only 1 in 10; and one with 3,000 workers of whom 382 were skilled had 41 apprentices—a proportion of 1 to 20. To how slight an extent the larger firms were taking their share in training can be seen from the following:

Total no. of employees	Adult skilled men	Apprentices
24,000	5,525	87
13,400	2,700	278
5,000	not stated	26
5,000	not stated	12
3,000	327	25
3,000	382	41
1,800	not stated	62
1,360	436	133
1,300	547	96
1,100	336	59
1,000	not stated	36
1,000	261	48
900	not stated	12
600	268	36
560	205	26
500	289	6
490	250	31

These are not picked out as exceptional but comprise the whole sample in this size group, and presumably are typical. They show the small amount of training undertaken by these firms.

About two-thirds of all the firms sending replies experienced serious shortages, of skilled men, particularly amongst bricklayers, plumbers, and carpenters and joiners, though a few firms reported that they had more of this last group available than they needed. These shortages were mentioned by firms of all sizes though they were stressed particularly by the larger firms, where the difficulty in getting enough bricklayers and carpenters was specially emphasized. That the trouble comes primarily from the lack of openings for apprentices is evidenced by the fact that hardly any of the firms had unfilled vacancies for apprentices. Where there were such unfilled openings they were generally for bricklayers, but even here it was only a small minority of firms in any size group that was affected. At the same time, unlike firms in the engineering and shipbuilding group of industries, very few firms had waiting lists of boys awaiting their turn to be apprenticed; and it is probable that the knowledge that the number of vacancies likely to become available is small, influenced boys (and their advisers) who might otherwise have been attracted to these crafts, but who are permanently lost to the industry, at least in the capacity of trained and qualified workers. Perhaps some of these attach themselves to firms in a non-apprentice capacity and later infiltrate into the skilled adult jobs, as described above. That this is at least a possibility is shown by the comparatively high figure (67%) recorded by the Ministry of Labour of boys of 15–17 years of age entering building and contracting as 'apprentices to a skilled craft' (out of 29,600 boys of this age, 20,700 were recorded as following an apprenticeship).[1] The Ministry of Labour's instruction to its local officers is to include in its statistics all those undergoing training of at least three years' duration, and this means that a number get included who are not serving an apprenticeship as laid down by the agreed scheme, or as the term is generally understood.

That the terms of the agreement are taken seriously by those employers who do train apprentices is shown by the fact that nearly 90% of the apprentices in the firms making returns were serving under written indenture, and in an outstanding majority of firms a certificate is granted when the apprenticeship is completed. It may be that this statement is over-optimistic, for it should be pointed out that a large number of firms failed to answer this question, and it is

[1] *Ministry of Labour Gazette*, October, 1956

likely that those with indentured apprentices replied more often than those without. The likelihood that there is a bias in this return is corroborated by the records of the Ministry of Works Census in 1953, which showed that only 56% of apprentices were serving under written indenture, and that in some regions, particularly those in the North, it was as low as 24% whereas in London and the Southern areas it was over 80%.[1]

With regard to the training itself the position is the same as was reported in the engineering and shipbuilding industries. With the exception of the technical instruction given during the time spent in the technical colleges the trainee is expected to acquire his skill by observation and practice. Only about half a dozen firms claimed to provide any supervision at all for their apprentices while they were at work, and it is fairly obvious that, considering the character of the greater part of building and maintenance work, it would be extremely difficult to arrange any form of specific instruction.

PRINTING

The printing industry has existed for 500 years but it is only in the last century or so that there have been introduced any profound changes in techniques. Unlike other skilled trades it has always demanded in addition to a high degree of manual skill, a certain standard of literacy. For a very long time, therefore, it could attract only those who had had some opportunity to be educated, and the level of skill demanded in the craft led to an insistence on an apprenticeship lasting seven years. Right up to the beginning of the last century the local trade clubs refused membership and employment to anybody who had not travelled the traditional path. But from the middle of the century matters rapidly changed. It was not that the changes in method called for any less knowledge or skill for the highest quality work than before, but that the industry spread so rapidly that it was no longer possible to control training or regulate entry. The capital required for a small hand

[1] Memorandum of Ministry of Works Census, May, 1953.

press was not very much more than could fairly easily be accumulated by many workers, so that there sprang up a large number of small firms, employing only one or two helpers; and the rapid growth of industry and trade needing bill-heads, advertisements, posters, invoices, price cards and a whole host of other small items, offered an expanding market for their work all over the country. Before this quick growth took place the printing industry had been confined to half a dozen large centres, where books and newspapers or other periodicals were printed and this concentration made control comparatively simple. But the proliferation of small businesses all over the new areas defied any attempt at regulation. Trade Union organization was practically unknown amongst these workers, many of whom were young boys. The standard of workmanship was extremely low, for the small local shopkeepers and manufacturers made no very exacting demands, provided their bills and posters were cheap and reasonably legible; but the youth who picked up in this way some elementary knowledge of typesetting could later move to a bigger firm as an 'improver' and so gradually drift into employment from which formerly he would have been rigorously excluded unless he had served his full time as an apprentice. The well-established compositors' unions in the big centres strove their utmost to maintain their control by insisting on apprenticeship for all young men employed by the big firms and by refusing admission to apprenticeship to any but a tiny proportion of the adult skilled force employed. As with the engineers the chief object of limitation was— as the Rules put it in 1867—'to adjust the balance of supply and demand and maintain a fair remuneration for labour' [1] rather than the belief that the craft could not be learned in a shorter period or with large numbers under training. But these restrictive practices operated exactly contrary to their intention, for the number of apprentices permitted by the unions was so grotesquely inadequate to the needs of an expanding industry that firms were forced to look for their additional workers from amongst those who had been employed in small establishments in uncontrolled towns and

[1] A. E. Musson, *The Typographical Association*, p. 210.

rural areas where the merest smattering of training had been provided. In order to prevent undercutting of wage rates by these unorganized and untrained workers the unions, by the end of the last century, had had to open their doors to any compositor who actually obtained employment with 'a fair house' whether he could show evidence of apprenticeship or not.[1] Even the large firms that were anxious to maintain a high standard of workmanship and were therefore ready to comply with the unions' demands, found these restrictions so rigid that they repeatedly raised the matter during negotiation between masters and unions; but the unions refused to alter. 'The Apprentice Rule became in effect a Typographical Association totem—quite useless but regarded with a kind of superstitious veneration as an ancient palladium against all ills—against unemployment, low wages, illegal men and incompetence'.[2] Many of the members realized the inelastic and arbitrary nature of their rules and that they did not even offer the protection intended. Even in towns where trade union organization was strong the rules were continually evaded in practice, particularly during periods of unemployment. But the Union refused to budge and this led to a slower growth of organization in the areas where the industry was newly establishing itself than would otherwise have been likely.

When the Webbs wrote their classic survey of trade unionism in the 'nineties there were only 40,000 members in the various printing unions; and they played an unimportant part in the movement as a whole. But the far-seeing minority who had begun to realize that exclusiveness was unlikely to gain the objects they desired while so much of the work could be done—whether well or badly—by untrained men, gradually began to gain ascendancy and a movement developed for some co-ordinating link, that would not only draw together the separate craft unions but would also cater for the less highly qualified men whose low pay, whilst they remained unorganized, was a constant threat to union agreements. In 1890 the craft unions formed the Printing and Kindred Trades Federation which a few years later opened

---

[1] S. & B. Webbs, *Industrial Democracy*, p. 464 ff.
[2] A. E. Musson, *The Typographical Association*, p. 214.

its doors to the newly-founded semi-skilled unions; it now has affiliated to it all the 16 unions in the industry with a total membership of over 320,000. For a long time the Federation had little power, for the constituent unions feared that their own particular problems might be overlooked if anything approaching full amalgamation was achieved. This has remained the constant fear of the craft unions which have retained, to a greater extent than in most other occupations where amalgamations have developed, autonomous control over their rates of pay and conditions of employment. But confidence has grown with the passing years, and many important matters dealing with such subjects as hours and holidays and apprentices' wages are now negotiated by the Federation. Although the unions have maintained their separate rights to negotiate wages and working conditions, they do agree to co-operate from time to time in collective approaches to the employers. The Federation acts by agreement on behalf of the unions in matters of common policy, and also has machinery for dealing with inter-union disputes.

The twentieth century saw a big development in trade union organization generally and the printing unions reflected this development. By the early 'twenties membership of those affiliated to the Federation had risen to 165,000, and this made it easier to maintain control of apprentices, particularly when the constituent unions opened their doors to those still under training, in order, as they said, 'to give them an early understanding of trade union principles'. But while the spread of organization resulted in a smaller number of unregulated firms it did not weaken the unions' decision to restrict apprenticeship; it merely made restrictions more effective. Throughout the period between the two wars the employers' associations continually asked for an increased ratio to be allowed, but without any effect, for the unions could point to the heavy percentage of unemployment with which they were already coping as a result of the prolonged depression, and insist that a relaxation of their rules would do no more than burden them with a larger number of skilled men to be maintained on the funds.

During the recent war circumstances conspired to give the

Federation more power and cohesion, for there were many problems affecting the whole industry, and in order to save time and prevent the confusion that might have resulted from separate negotiations with 16 unions, the Federation undertook to make war emergency agreements with the Government to which all submitted. As many men as possible had to be released for war production as well as for active service, and agreements had to be made for others—women or younger people—to take on their work. As the Federation negotiated with the Government on behalf of its constituent bodies on all these special problems its influence and authority were more widely acknowledged and by the end of the war it had achieved a much greater degree of power than it had previously enjoyed.

Already two years before the war the craft unions with apprentice members had made some efforts to improve the unsatisfactory situation in which their apprentices usually found themselves. There were no agreed wage scales for apprentices and this resulted in widely varying and sometimes extremely low rates of pay. The unions came to the conclusion that it was unlikely that any real improvement would be made unless they all acted together, and they were in the middle of negotiations on this matter when war broke out and other problems took the front of the stage. It was not until 1943 that the first general wages agreement for apprentices was signed, and this agreement remained virtually unchanged until 1956. It provided that the apprentice should receive a percentage of the appropriate journeyman's wage increasing from 20% in the first year to 60% in the last.

In 1956 new scales for apprentices were agreed as follows:

Period of apprenticeship		Percentage of minimum wage of journeymen
6 years	5 years	
1	—	25
2	1	30
3	2	40
4	3	55
5	4	65
6	5	75

A further agreement provided that half the time spent in the Services by those called up whilst still in training should be counted towards the completion of their apprenticeship and that they should continue to be ranked as on the roll of apprentices of their employing firms whilst they were away. This meant that a firm that had its full ratio of apprentices (as described below) could not take on another trainee whilst those nominally serving an apprenticeship with it were away on service or essential war production.

Meanwhile, in common with other industries, the Joint Industrial Council for the Printing Industry was discussing the Memorandum on the Selection and Training of Juveniles that the Ministry of Labour had circulated in 1942, and in 1945 it issued its agreed scheme. The main clauses were as follows:

(1) A standard form of indenture should be adopted throughout the industry and signed by the employer, the boy and his guardian.

(2) All apprentices should be released for one day each week to attend technical instruction not merely up to the age of 18 but until completion of apprenticeship. In addition all those over 18 should be expected to attend evening classes, though for the ones younger than this such attendance should be voluntary.

(3) A National Certificate should be instituted in order to provide a credential which would be universally recognized as guaranteeing competence. This Certificate, which would not be awarded until the apprenticeship had been completed, would be based on the record of progress throughout the whole period of training, and on the results of an examination conducted by the technical college. A high proportion of the marks in this examination would be given for practical work.

In addition a Certificate of Completed Apprenticeship was to be instituted. This would be signed by the employer and endorsed by the Local Apprenticeship Committee.

(4) The scheme was to be administered by a nationally constituted Apprentice Authority assisted by Local Apprenticeship Committees set up throughout the industry as

sub-committees of the District Committees of the Joint Industrial Council for the Printing Industry. A novel feature of this scheme, and one in which the industry differs from others, is that the Local Apprenticeship Committees are given the task of selecting suitable recruits for apprenticeship on the basis of educational and psychological tests, and after a medical examination of the applicant. It was suggested that school reports and health records obtained through the co-operation of the Youth Employment Service be taken into account, and that wherever possible a psychologist be appointed to help in selection.

It was recommended that no boy be indentured to an employer until he had been examined and accepted by the Committee; and that no employer be allowed to engage an apprentice unless the Committee believed the firm to offer reasonable opportunities and equipment for training.

(5) Unlike most other skilled trades the usual term of apprenticeship in printing has always been seven years, though some sections of the industry had made agreements which permitted a reduction of one year for those who remained at a secondary or technical school until 15, or of two years for those who remained until 16. It was now recommended that in view of the raising of the school-leaving age consideration should be given to a general reduction of the period of apprenticeship to five years ending at 21, and to a review of existing quotas of apprentices in the different crafts.

(6) The crafts for which apprenticeship is demanded are:

Compositors	Electrotypers
Lithographic Artists	Photogravure Process Workers
„ Printers	Plate and Cylinder Product
Monotype Caster	Tradesmen
Operatives	Letterpress Machine Workers
Stereotypers	Bookbinders.

It will be noticed that in this scheme it was suggested that the ratio of apprentices to journeymen be reviewed in the light of the new labour situation caused by the raising of the school-leaving age and the introduction of day release, but no figure was suggested because this is a matter on which the various unions have autonomy. In fact, despite this general recommendation, the unions have continued to maintain a more rigid insistence on restricted entry to the trade than is found in any other of the occupations included in this enquiry, with the possible exception of welders.

This may be due to the fact that unlike all the other industries under review the personnel of printing was forcibly reduced during the war years, and its male employees who numbered 199,000 in 1939 were only 97,000 at the end of the war. True that a year later, with the return of the men from the Forces, this figure bounded up to 156,000, but despite this expansion those in the industry were not sure of the future. The restrictions on the import of paper were so great that it seemed unlikely that there would be any great immediate development, and the unions feared that an increase in the number of apprentices would shortly face them with such a large supply of skilled men that it would be impossible for them to find regular employment or to maintain their rates of pay.

A factor which makes the control of entry more restricted is that the number admitted is not proportionate to the total numbers employed. The permitted intake of apprentices is very much smaller for the larger firm than it is for the small establishment. The ratios now agreed with the various craft unions are shown in the table on the next page.

As regards the term of apprenticeship, it was agreed that this should be reduced from 7 years to 6 as long as the school-leaving age remains at 15 but that this should include any period of compulsory National Service begun either at the normal time or after deferment, provided that no apprenticeship ends before 21 and that it allows at least five years' actual craft training.

The Apprentice Authority was duly set up and in 1947 it issued a Memorandum of guidance to its Local Apprenticeship Committees which set forth the principles on which the selection of recruits should be made, and which suggested suitable programmes for workshop training. It naturally took a little time for the scheme to get into its stride

Number of Journeymen Employed

No. of Apprentices	Typographical Association			Book Binders and Machine Rulers	Electrotypers and Stereotypers Society		Litho Printers Society	Litho Artists, etc. Society
	Letterpress Composing Room	Letterpress Machine Room	Monotype Caster Operators		Jobbing and Weekly news	Newspaper Foundries		
1	1 to 2 (a)	2 to 3	1 to 2	1 to 4	3 to 5	—	1 to 5	1 to 4
2	3 to 7	4 to 7	3 to 7	5 to 9	6 to 8	1 to 11	6 to 10	5 to 8
3	8 to 17 (b)	8 to 17	8 to 17	10 to 14	9 to 11	12 to 15	11 to 15	9 to 12
4	18 to 39	18 to 39	18 and over	15 to 19	12 to 16	16 to 19	16 to 20	13 to 16
5	40 to 59	40 to 59		20 to 24	17 to 21	20 to 23	21 to 25	17 to 20
6	60 to 79	60 to 79		25 to 29	22 and over	24 and over	26 to 30	
7	80 to 99	80 to 99		30 to 34			31 to 35	
8				35 to 39			36 to 59	
9	and one additional apprentice for each additional 1 to 20 journeymen	and one additional apprentice for each additional 1 to 20 journeymen		40 to 49			60 to 79	
10				50 to 59			80 to 100 and over	
11	(a) fully employed 6 months			60 to 79				
12	(b) fully employed 12 months			80 to 99				
				and one additional apprentice for each additional 1 to 20 journeymen thereafter				and one additional apprentice for each additional 1 to 4 journeymen thereafter

but, unlike the engineering and shipbuilding industries, the National Body was not content to issue its scheme, sit back and hope for the best. It took steps to find out how far its proposals had been accepted and acted upon. The question of the Recruitment and Training of Personnel for the Industry was the main item on the agenda of the Annual Conference of the Joint Industrial Council held at Nottingham in November, 1953, and this provided an opportunity for a review of the scheme up to that date by Mr. G. G. Eastwood, Assistant General Secretary of the Printing and Kindred Trades Federation, based on enquiries he had made amongst the J.I.C. District Committees all over the country.

Although the scheme had been generally approved, not all the District Committees had by that time implemented it; but in 44 out of the 73 District Committees of the Federation (and these included most of the large towns and cities) schemes were in fact in operation. Methods however varied considerably. In 7 areas boys presenting themselves for approval by the Local Apprenticeship Committees were sponsored by member firms, and although there was no regulation against the application of an unsponsored boy direct to the Committee, he had in practice little chance of being examined or accepted. In London, for example, the largest centre for printing, including 37% of the total personnel in the industry, 1,349 boys sponsored by employers were examined by the Committee during the period 1949–53. During this same period 6,301 boys who were not sponsored intimated a desire to be considered for the industry, but only 976 boys were able to be examined. On the other hand, in other areas boys applied direct to the Committee on their own initiative or had their names supplied by the Youth Employment Officer and, having passed the test set by the Committee, were recommended to an employer by whom the final choice was made.

There have of course been difficulties on both sides in agreeing to accept the selection of an impartial body. The employer has always before had the right to select whomsoever he pleased without consulting any other judge than himself about suitability; and workers who often had had the right to present their sons for an apprenticeship vacancy were disconcerted to find that the boys had to be tested by a committee which might turn them down. In the large majority of districts where the scheme was in operation employers loyally accepted the decision of the Local Apprenticeship Committee but there were certain cases reported of employers engaging an apprentice, despite the fact that he had been rejected by the Committee, and this led to great dissatisfaction. In other cases employers engaged apprentices themselves and then sent them to be interviewed after they had already committed themselves and when the Committee's opinion could have little practical effect.

An important and novel item in the printing scheme was the recommendation that no boy should be accepted without a medical examination and without submitting to educational and psychological tests; but this provision has not been included in all the local schemes. Some committees sensibly deferred the medical examination until the boy had proved himself satisfactory in the other tests, but a considerable number cut it out altogether because the employers were unwilling to pay the cost. The education and psychological tests are more general and are carried out, sometimes by the members of the local committees in co-operation with the Youth Employment Officers, and sometimes by local schoolmasters, or instructors from the printing department of the local technical college. When the scheme was inaugurated the importance of intelligence tests was much emphasized and committees were given advice as to how well-known tests might be applied; but it is still a comparative minority that have implemented this recommendation. The London Bookbinders' Committee send their candidates for apprenticeship to the National Institute of Industrial Psychology for examination in aptitudes, and appear to be very satisfied with the results; intelligence and vocational tests have been included in the Glasgow scheme; and the Edinburgh Master Printers' Association gets the co-operation of the Department of Psychology of the University of Edinburgh in its selection.

Having selected suitable apprentices, how far do the Committees ensure that they receive the graded course of training laid down in the scheme? According to Mr. Eastwood's survey, only just half of the local committees which were actually operating schemes are supplied with periodical progress reports, and if the whole country is taken into account, in 75% of the districts no more is heard of the apprentice throughout his training, once he is indentured, unless some serious difficulty occurs. Nor is there any serious supervision of workshop training. In only four districts was there definite information that the scheme of training was in operation, and though the Workshop Training Booklet had recommended 'that each apprentice should from the commencement of his apprenticeship be placed under the guidance of a journeyman selected as much for his understanding and patience as for his craft knowledge', Eastwood was able to find only one place where this had been adopted in the way that had been intended.

The information collected during the enquiry fully corroborates the impression of the survey summarized above. The replies covered a particularly high proportion of the industry, for in London and the South-East Region in which 37% of the whole labour force of the industry is employed, returns came from over 86% of the firms circulated, and in other areas in which there are considerable concentrations of the industry, i.e. Yorkshire, North-West, Scotland and the Eastern areas, the proportion varied from 62 to 75%.

While there are a number of well-known and very large firms in the industry, there are also an extremely large number of small establishments; in fact, 31% of the personnel is employed in firms with less than 50 employees and 15% in firms with 50–100 workers. As regards these size categories the smallest firms are less represented in returns, for whereas the replies from firms with over 100 employees were 82%, and with those in the middle grade 100%, it was only 53% of the smallest establishments who returned the questionnaire.

Of the smallest firms nearly one quarter of those making returns had no apprentices at all, many of them explaining that they would be glad to engage them but find the restrictions too onerous. As the ratio for the small firms is very much more generous than for the larger employers, this results in a significant reduction of the total number of apprentices attached to the industry. This was a matter for continual comment during the enquiry. Many employers interviewed expressed the view that the maintenance of the ratio would be much less burdensome if it could be related to the employment situation of a whole locality instead of the position in an individual firm. The larger firms with up-to-date methods and a wide diversity of work in hand are prevented from training more than a comparatively small number and are not allowed to take up the slack of the small firms who, often enough, cannot afford the number of apprentices allowed them by the ratio. The situation is completely changed from the times when the small firm tried to take on as many boy workers as it could, because wages were so low. In the early years of this century a boy was paid 5s. a week when he began his apprenticeship and advanced by 2s. a year until he received 17s. at the end of his 7-year period.[1] But since the introduction of the National Agreement controlling the pay of apprentices boys are no longer cheap labour, particularly in view of the expense to which the employer is put in the payment of technical college fees, and the payment of wages during day release, and many small firms cannot afford apprentices whose employment faces them with continual interruption to their work during class hours. Nor can the industry any longer rely on attracting a very large number of applicants. As it is mainly concentrated in areas in which there are many competing openings the small firm has little to offer to draw suitable boys to it as apprentices.

How seriously this method of calculating the ratio affects the lads under training can be seen from a more detailed study of the firms included in the returns. The 51 firms with less than 50 employees each employ between them a total of 393 skilled adult craftsmen, spread over all the various crafts in the industry. As shown above each craft has its own rules. The Typographical Association, by far the largest single craft union in the industry, allows 1 apprentice for every 2 compositors or monotype caster operatives and 1 apprentice for 3 letterpress machine workers, and the other craft unions

[1] Ellic Howe and H. E. Waite, *The London Society of Compositors*, p. 314.

covering very much smaller groups allow 1 apprentice to 3, 4 or 5 adults. One could expect therefore a total of about 175 apprentices in all crafts attached to these firms. In fact, there were only 107, a proportion of very little more than 1 : 4.

In the large firms a ratio of only 1 to every 20 journeymen over 100 is allowed. In the four largest firms in the enquiry, each with over 1,000 employees, there were 1,552 skilled adult craftsmen with only 221 apprentices amongst them all.

The consequent serious shortage of skilled workers was a matter that came continually under discussion during interviews, and many firms, in addition, pointed out that with the present age structure of the labour force the position was likely to get increasingly serious. Already it is often difficult to replace workers who reach retiring age, and in the very near future the proportion of the total labour force in this position will be increasingly large. In 1950 the proportion of men in the industry over 60 years of age was about 10%; by the end of 1953 it was $11\frac{1}{2}\%$, and of this $11\frac{1}{2}\%$ nearly half were over 65.[1]

Further difficulty arises from the fact that newspaper presses employ very large numbers of highly skilled men, but the nature of their work and the hours during which it must be carried on, do not allow them to be responsible for anything like the number of apprentices proportionate to their adult labour force. They must therefore draw from the pool of craftsmen trained in other firms, whose number of apprentices are not sufficient even for their own requirements, and as the newspapers usually pay higher rates than general printing firms they are able to attract staff, which leaves those who have had the burden of training them in difficulties. Hardly any firms included in the enquiry expressed themselves as satisfied with the position and the outstanding majority in all size groups recorded special shortages of compositors and letterpress machine workers.

At the end of the war the ratio was temporarily suspended to allow the block intake of apprentices so as to help to

---

[1] A speech by Mr. R. A. Jackson, Chairman of the Labour Sub-Committee of the British Federation of Master Printers, at a Conference with the District Association, January, 1954.

make good the deficiency which resulted from nearly six years of war during which very few apprenticeships had been begun. But the number allowed fell far short of those lost throughout the war years. In one craft alone, that of compositors, it was calculated that 4,000 fewer apprentices had been admitted between 1939 and 1945 than would have entered the industry in peacetime, while the block intakes permitted by the unions amounted to only 500. In addition the break of two years of National Service reduces the number of skilled journeymen available, so that by that factor alone the craft has to face a loss of output of about 1,000 men. In a Conference held between the British Federation of Master Printers and the Typographical Association, in order to allow the Master Printers to urge on the union the importance of some relaxation of the rigid ratio, Mr. R. A. Jackson calculated that there was a deficiency of about 6,000 men amongst compositors, monotype casters and letterpress workers amounting to about 16% of the journeyman strength in these crafts. In begging for increased recruitment to be allowed, he pointed out that the unions were in no danger of flooding the market with more skilled men than the industry could absorb because the agreements already entered into by the employers were their safeguards. The first provision was that dilutees who had been admitted during the war should be dismissed first if any question of redundancy arose. The second provided for the reduction of weekly hours to $42\frac{1}{2}$ as soon as sufficient labour was available; and the third, a clause in an agreement in 1951, provided that earlier retirement should be encouraged, and the intake of apprentices be reduced should the figure of unemployment reach 4%. The Typographical Association, however, were unwilling to relax their restrictions. They agreed that there was indeed a labour shortage at the moment but they felt that there was no guarantee that serious unemployment might not occur again in the future. During the inter-war years the union had spent £50,000 a year on unemployment benefit, and it was determined not to take any action that might involve it in a risk of having to meet such an emergency again.

Matters were brought to a head as a result of a prolonged

strike which took place in London in April, 1956. The dispute was not a national one but concerned only the London section of the industry, which is separately organized from that of the Provinces. The dispute was a continuation of a difference of opinion that had taken place five years earlier when a Court of Inquiry set up by the Ministry of Labour and National Service to investigate the situation recommended that, on account of the shortage of skilled workers, provision should be made under adequate safeguards for the admission of adult trainees. It also proposed that there should be a periodical adjustment by a Joint Committee of the industry of the ratio of apprentices in the light of the employment situation. The agreement which followed publication of this report provided for a block intake of 220 apprentices who were to be introduced as far as practicable within the following twelve months, in addition to a change in the normal ratio of apprentices from 1 : 4 to 1 : 3, and a reduction of the period of apprenticeship from 7 to 6 years. The reduction in the length of training did in fact take place but the increase in apprentice intake was not as large as had been hoped. Both parties had agreed that these terms should remain for a period of five years and it was at the end of this time that the unions put forward demands for a considerable increase in wage rates. This demand was opposed by the employers, a deadlock ensued and a further Court of Enquiry was set up which reported in March, 1956.[1]

The employers' case was that the unions' insistence on the rigid ratios was primarily maintained in order to allow them to push up wage rates and the resulting increase to the costs of the firms were so heavy that they were being priced out of the market. A great many large firms in other industries were setting up their own presses to meet their own domestic requirements, and as their operators did not come under printing unions' jurisdiction, they were able to operate at lower costs. In addition, an increasing amount of work was being sent abroad. They believed that the unions' fear of unemployment was greatly exaggerated, unless indeed they created it by their own action, but in any case the Master

[1] Cmd. Paper 9717.

Printers were prepared to discuss ways of dealing with un-employment as soon as it arose.

The Union on the other hand insisted that unemployment would be a serious menace if the number of skilled workers was allowed to increase too rapidly. It pointed out that its responsibility to its members for unemployment and super-annuation pay was lifelong, and it dared not risk having on its books any large number of men unable to get regular jobs or forced to early retirement. As a *quid pro quo* for a higher wage however, it offered some relaxation of apprenticeship ratios which would permit a block intake of 200 apprentices be-tween the ages of 21 and 25 who should be subject to only four years' apprenticeship training, and in addition, the admission of apprentices at a ratio of 1 : 3 with a more liberal interpretation of the type of journeyman who should count in the calculation.

The Report came to the conclusion that there was indeed a serious manpower shortage though it could not assess this with any exactness. It pointed out however that during the five years that the last agreement had been in operation there had been virtually no unemployment at all, and that the average monthly hours of overtime that it had been found necessary to work had increased from 100,000 to 160,000. These two facts taken together could be con-sidered evidence of a real shortage, and it recommended that an increase in both adult and junior apprentices be allowed.

In the following month a new agreement was made be-tween the British Federation of Master Printers, the News-paper Society and the London Master Printers' Association, with the four unions, the Typographical Association, the Amalgamated Society of Lithoprinters, the London Typo-graphical Society and the Association of Correctors of the Press.

This amended the appropriate ratios as follows:
The Typographical Association:

(1) A block of 545 bonus apprentices in composing and letterpress machine departments, to be introduced in three annual instalments of 245, 150 and 150.

(2) Present normal quotas to continue except that mono-caster departments with three journeymen will be entitled to only 1 apprentice.

Amalgamated Society of Lithoprinters:

The apprentice quotas to be amended to the following:

(a) 1 apprentice to 4 journeymen up to 32 journeymen.
9 apprentices—from 33 to 50 journeymen.
10 apprentices—from 51 to 70 journeymen.
11 apprentices—from 71 to 100 journeymen.
No establishment to have more than 11 apprentices.

(b) A block of 100 additional apprentices to be taken into the industry at the rate of 20 per annum beginning 1957.

(c) An annual transfer of 25 members of the M. and R. section (semi-skilled section) to full craft status subject to three years' training during which they would receive 90%, 92½% and 95% respectively of the minimum grade rate.

In (b) and (c) suitable candidates over the age of 18 to be accepted.

While there is this serious shortage of adult workers there is no shortage at all of applicants for apprenticeship. Hardly a single firm had an unfilled vacancy in the sense of experiencing difficulty in attracting young people, though half a dozen mentioned that they had in each case a single vacancy, as it happened that the enquiry arrived at the moment of selecting a new apprentice. In interviews indeed there were many representatives of employers' associations who said that, far from there being any shortage, it was difficult to choose, for there might be as many as 30 candidates for a single apprenticeship.

Before the great expansion and specialization of the printing industry took place during the first half of the last century apprentices were trained in all departments of the trade, and when they became journeymen they worked indiscriminately on one job or another. In the same way, when printing machines were introduced they became 'twicers' trained to both case and machine. But as the staff of firms increased and more complicated machines were introduced, specialization became more common and each department developed its own form of training. It was the employers who took the initiative in this, generally against the wish of the unions, who were reluctant to admit to membership persons they thought insufficiently trained; but as time went on and the various crafts developed their own separate union organization, strict rules were drawn up restricting the operation of various processes to those who had been trained as specialists in such jobs. Despite the establishment of the Printing and Kindred Trades Federation this rigid independence of the craft unions has remained a characteristic feature of the printing industry and it is not permitted to an apprentice to one craft to learn the work of another, or to an adult to move over the boundary lines dividing them.

In very large firms this clear-cut line of demarcation does not present any serious problem, for there must usually be a considerable number of each type of craftsman employed. It may happen occasionally that work is held up in some departments on account of a bottleneck in another process where the staff is short; but this is not a general state of affairs. The number of large firms in the industry is however a small proportion of the total for, as has been shown, 31% of the total labour force is employed in firms with less than 50 employees and it is here that this inflexibility leads to difficulties. The capital equipment of modern printing firms is extremely expensive and if it is not fully utilized the overhead charges become too heavy to be economic. The lack of a single man in one branch may prevent several others from carrying on their own work because they are not permitted to do any other jobs than the ones that fall within their own craft lines, although they might be able to tackle these quite competently. Indeed, it is widely believed that it would not be difficult for the average apprentice to acquire proficiency in two crafts during his period of training, but the reintroduction of such a system is prevented mainly by the fear of unemployment on the part of the craft unions, and partly by the fact that these all remain so determinedly autonomous in negotiating rates of pay and terms of employment.

An apprentice in the printing industry has the right of any other young man undergoing recognized training to ask for deferment from National Service until his training is complete. In most skilled industries full advantage is taken of this privilege but printing provides an exception. There were some firms that complained during interviews that 90% of the apprentices in the industry refused to ask for deferment and that this still further reduced their quota of trainees because, as an apprentice in the Services is counted as being still on the firm's books, his place could not be filled by another boy. Such a high percentage is not confirmed by the returns in the enquiry but these did offer evidence that the situation in printing is indeed markedly different from that of the other trades. In engineering and shipbuilding, for example, just as it is in building, it is rare for a boy to interrupt his apprenticeship to do his National Service. How many apprentices in the sample firms in printing took an opposite line it is impossible to say as a considerable number of firms did not reply to this question; but of those who did provide information, just about half reported that their apprentices had not asked for deferment.

At the time of Mr. Eastwood's survey of the progress of the scheme an insignificant number of Local Apprenticeship Committees could report that the carefully worked out scheme of workshop training, prepared as a guide to employers and local bodies, was in operation. This seems still to be the case. It is rare for a firm to have anybody specially responsible for the training of apprentices. The few firms large enough to have personnel managers naturally expect these officers to keep general watch over the welfare and progress of their trainees, but their particular function is in connection with the main labour force of adults. It may be that there are in fact some firms in the printing industry with well-organized Works Schools similar to those found so frequently in various sections of the engineering industry but they have not come to light during the course of this enquiry. For the most part the apprentice is put in the care of an adult craftsman and it is a matter of chance whether his teacher is an interested and capable teacher or not. Although great emphasis was laid in the Memorandum on the importance of supervision and good sympathetic teaching, little seems to have been done by most employers to provide it. One of the most famous Master Printers said, 'A great deal more could be done if employers understood the importance of *teaching* apprentices instead of leaving them to pick up their craft. The trouble at present is that the employer is too concerned with the loss of production by the person teaching and cannot see beyond the day's docket to realize that it is a capital investment for the boy to be better taught.' Whilst it is rare for boys to be kept on unproductive jobs as they used to be, because of the high wages they now receive, they are often kept on a narrow range of jobs on which they show proficiency, instead of being given the wide experience that a thorough training demands. Some employers may believe that any deficiency in this respect can be made good during the day on which the apprentice receives instruction at the technical college, but in the Report on the Recruitment and Training of Apprentices, both sides explicitly repudiated this view. It was there emphasized that sound instruction in practical methods of production under the competitive conditions governing the workshop is as important as the broad technical education and the regard for accuracy and right method which the technical college can provide; but the general impression is that this 'sound instruction in practical methods' is by no means universal or even common. Only three firms of those making returns in this enquiry could report that they provided any special supervision at all for their apprentices.

It may be that employers feel it is hardly worth the expense of providing more careful instruction for their apprentices if the standard of proficiency reached makes no difference to the length of training that they have to provide; for one way in which the shortage of skilled workers might be lessened whilst still retaining the ratio between apprentices and journeymen could be by shortening the period of training. If a boy could be fully trained in, say three years, instead of five, he could join the ranks of the journeymen at the age of 18 or when he returned from the Forces, thus leaving an apprenticeship vacancy to allow of another person being added to the total labour force.

How far a complete training can be provided in a shorter period of time is not a matter capable of statistical assessment without undertaking an experimental scheme, and this is not permitted by trade union regulations. The opinion however seems to be general that a boy could acquire proficiency in three or at most four years' time. The Head of a famous University Press, much of whose work is exceptionally expert (e.g. the setting of mathematics, scientific papers and foreign languages), gave it as his opinion that a boy could be taught to do any of this accurately in six months. He thought it would not be fair to the boy to do this, however, because, unless he were guaranteed lifelong employment in this work, he would find himself in difficulties if he wanted to move on to another firm. But with three years' training it was thought he could master a sufficient variety of types of work to be able to turn to any job within the scope of his craft.

How soon an apprentice becomes a net gain to the firm is again a matter of opinion. One employer said that the first two years were a loss, the next two 'break even', and the fifth and sixth were a definite gain; another said that an apprentice became of real value to the firm after the first year's training, and others held a position somewhere between these two. The Personnel Manager of one of the largest firms gave it as his opinion that if the period of apprenticeship were reduced to three years the firm would lose in having to pay adult wages instead of apprentice rates for the period in which they normally recouped themselves for the losses in which they had been involved in the first years, but that it would gain in the long run by having a skilled labour force that was more nearly adequate to the demand. The unions however are strongly opposed to any reduction in the period of training. They point out that an apprenticeship which used to be seven years in duration is now six, and this is in fact reduced to five years by the agreement which allows half the time in the Forces to be reckoned as part of the period of training. To reduce it still further is in their view out of the question.

THE MOTOR VEHICLE REPAIRING INDUSTRY

The motor vehicle repairing industry differs from the others included in this enquiry in two important respects. The first is that it is preponderantly composed of small units. Almost every village of any size has a filling station with a mechanic capable of carrying out the majority of the repairs needed by the customers; and in urban areas there is similar provision in every few streets. Often enough the proprietor himself is the skilled mechanic and with part-time help from, perhaps, other members of his family, or a couple of employees to help in looking after the petrol pump and washing cars, he is able to do all that is required.

In the section of the industry which thus combines repair work with running a filling station 24% of the labour force works in units that have less than five employees and only 2·5% in establishments with over 50 workers. In the section that deals only with repairs and has no pumps $27\frac{1}{2}$% work in firms with less than five employees and 47% in those with less than 10.

The second respect in which the industry differs from others is that it is comparatively new and has no tradition of apprenticeship or of other regulated entry to the trade. Although the work is highly skilled (for by its very nature there is no possibility of introducing mass production methods) there was no particular form of training demanded in the years before the war. Boys used to be taken on when they left school and they picked up their knowledge by observation, and by being given simple jobs to do. The main impetus for the introduction of the present scheme of training came from the recognition that, in a labour-hungry world such as could be expected after the war, there would be intense competition for the dwindling number of young people available, and that only those industries which could offer a scheme of progressive employment with increasing knowledge and responsibility, would have a chance of attracting the higher quality recruit. It was not only the anxiety about attracting additional workers, however, that motivated those who drew up the scheme of training; they felt also that they had a serious responsibility towards the public. Most owners of cars and motor cycles have a very rudimentary knowledge of the mechanism. A number can probably apply a few standard tests to enable them to guess why a car will not start, but few go beyond that point, and when they bring a vehicle for repair or readjustment they must put themselves in the hands of the firm, and accept its judgment on what needs to be done. Whether the diagnosis made by the mechanic is correct, and whether the right remedial action has been taken, can often not be judged by the customer for a considerable period of time. It is essential therefore that he should feel confidence in those advising him, and the industry believed that it would be to its long-term advantage to provide for its mechanics a thorough training, which would carry a recognized credential as guarantee.

The scheme for this industry therefore, like that in the printing industry, provides for the grant of a Certificate which requires the apprentice not simply to complete the period of apprenticeship but also to pass an examination which shows he has reached a certain standard of competence. Unlike that suggested for the printing industry, however, it lays down in the agreed Memorandum what that standard should be, and provides that the examination shall be conducted, at least in part, by an outside body.

The National Craftsman's Certificate for Motor Vehicle Service Mechanics is only awarded on three conditions, all of which must be fulfilled:

(i) The satisfactory completion of an approved three years' part-time motor mechanics' course at a technical college or school.

(ii) A pass in the City and Guilds of London Institute Intermediate examination in Motor Mechanics taken at the end of this course.

(iii) A pass in the trade's own examination in practical work taken in the last year of a normal five years' apprenticeship or after having had equivalent experience.

The apprentice is not allowed to offer himself for the trade's examination, which is held once a year, until he has fulfilled the first two conditions. Recognition of the standard of skill and knowledge implied by possession of this credential is shown by the fact that if he gets the Certificate before he goes into the Services and is posted to R.E.M.E. or the R.A.F. he is entitled to be allowed to forgo the sixteen weeks' initial training generally required before one is placed in the Vehicle Mechanics' category.

The examination is conducted by the Joint Industrial Council for the industry on which the Motor Agents' Association, which includes about 83% of the firms within its scope, represents the employers, and the workers are represented by the Amalgamated Engineering Union, the Electrical Trades Union, the National Union of Vehicle Builders, the Transport and General Workers' Union and the National Union of General and Municipal Workers; and the fact that the trade itself is responsible for this final credential has had as one of its most important consequences the fact that the industry has taken a much more active part in supervising apprenticeship than has been shown by the National Body in any other industry included in this Survey.

At the end of 1955 there were known to be 17,730 apprentices employed by the members of the M.A.A. in relation to the total labour force of 171,000, of whom 40,010 were skilled men. In addition there were 21,840 working directors and proprietors, a good proportion of whom (though *what* proportion is not known) were skilled mechanics. Not all of the apprentices were in fact attending technical classes (see Chapter V) but over a period of five years 90% of those in the third year of the Motor Mechanics' course actually sat for the City and Guilds Institute examination (an exceptionally high proportion in comparison with other skilled industries) and of these, on an average 52% passed. Not all of those who were successful in the City and Guilds examination were eligible under the strict rules of the Joint Industrial Council to sit for the National Craftsman's Certificate. The City and Guilds examination may be taken in certain circumstances by boys who train overseas, or by those who are not within reach of school or college and prepare themselves by correspondence courses. Neither of these two categories is permitted to sit for the National Craftsman's Certificate. There were some however who were eligible but who, in their own words, 'could not bother' or 'didn't think it worth while'; so that actually only 65% of those who were successful in City and Guilds took the extra credential. By the end of 1955 3,500 National Craftsman's Certificates had been awarded, and as the number of entries had risen each year, it seemed probable that the entries for 1956 would be over 1,000.

In other respects the scheme for the Motor Vehicle Repairing Industry follows the usual pattern. Apprenticeship is for five years beginning at 16, and provides for Day Release to attend technical classes for three years. As with building and printing, emphasis is laid on the importance of registering the apprentice with a National Body; and the industry seems to be singularly successful in persuading its employer members to fulfil this part of their obligations. During 1953, for example, 2,611 apprentices were registered, and from the beginning of the scheme in January, 1947, there were a total of 20,401 registrations. As all of those who started their training at the commencement of the scheme must have completed it before 1955 it appears from a comparison of this total with the number of apprentices then under training (17,730) that an outstanding majority of apprentices must be registered with the National Body.

No ratio of apprentices to journeymen is laid down, nor is there any provision for local regulations on this matter; but the fact that the National Body has a record of the majority of apprenticeships entered into, enables it to keep an eye on the situation, should the need arise. At present, so far as the results of this enquiry go, so large a proportion of firms are unwilling to train apprentices that the main concern of those in control of the scheme is to find ways of increasing the number under training rather than of devising methods for keeping boys out. Booklets setting forth the attractions of skilled work in the industry have been issued, and close co-operation with the Youth Employment Service is urged on all local officers, so as to ensure that as many as possible of school-leavers are made aware of the openings available.

The crafts to which boys can be apprenticed are:

(*a*)   Mechanics
(*b*)   Auto Electricians
(*c*)   Panel Beaters
(*d*)   Painters and Sprayers
(*e*)   Plasterers
(*f*)   Upholsterers
(*g*)   Carpenters and Joiners
(*h*)   Coach Builders.

Wages are fixed as a percentage of the appropriate skilled rate:

Age	Proportion
15	25%
16	30%
17	40%
18	50%
19	60%
20	75%

The industry is, as has been said, spread over the whole country; but not all areas are equally represented in the returns to the enquiry. From London and the South-East and from the South-West area there were 85% returns and from the Midlands, the North-West, Yorkshire and Scotland replies varied from 63 to 70%, but there were no replies at all from Wales and only 25% from the Northern and Eastern Regions. Fortunately, the areas with the highest returns are also those with the largest number of establishments.

As with all other industries in this enquiry the burden of training the new recruits is very unevenly borne. Of the firms with under 10 employees 62% had no apprentices at all, and of those with less than 5 the proportion was even larger. But a very considerable number added the comment that they would eagerly take on apprentices if boys of suitable quality presented themselves. In the next large category, those employing between 10 and 50 workers, there were just under a third who had no apprentices, and the others varied very greatly. There were a few with as many apprentices as skilled adults, for example, 3 apprentices to 4 men or 3 apprentices to 3 men; but on the other hand there were firms with 17 skilled men and only 1 apprentice, and others with 12–14 skilled adults and 2 apprentices. More often than in any other group in any other industry, firms added comments about the difficulty of getting the numbers of suitable boys they would like, and only one firm said '. . . cannot afford the time and trouble to train apprentices'. Even the largest firms experienced some difficulty. One wrote 'This firm has employed and trained apprentices in the post-war years, but their experience has not been very satisfactory. Apprentices have left before finishing their time because of the highly competitive jobs in the surrounding industries, and the boys have not been all that keen, nor of really good enough quality, and so on. The work has tended to become more specialized, and we simply cannot afford the time required to devote to training especially with the danger of most, if not all, eventually leaving the firm.' There were several other comments of a like nature.

Yet the shortage of skilled workers is acute. Only one-sixth of the firms replying were satisfied with the position, almost all the others complaining in particular of the shortage of mechanics. Panel beaters and auto electricians were also in short supply but nothing like to the same extent as mechanics.

In common with the majority of firms in other industries training is purely 'on the job', apart from the instruction given in the technical colleges. It is not surprising that in an industry that is composed almost entirely of small firms it is impossible to provide any special training section in the works, or to appoint any person to be primarily responsible for training young workers, and skill is therefore picked up by watching others and by attempting to tackle the job oneself.

What emerges from this Survey? That there is an acute shortage of skilled workers is not in doubt. It is shown by the constant high figure of unfilled vacancies for craftsmen and it is confirmed by the replies to the questionnaires. But with the exception of the printing industry where the craft unions maintain a stranglehold over the intake of apprentices, and of some local sections of the shipbuilding industry, this shortage is not the result of any excessive restriction of entry on the part of the unions. It may be true, as many firms have suggested in the course of discussion, that the difficulty might be overcome, at least in part, if there were not such rigid lines of demarcation between groups of workers. Technological changes have altered the nature of certain jobs to such an extent that they no longer need the level of skill assumed by a five-year apprenticeship; but there still remains the intense opposition of skilled workers to any attempt to shift these jobs into the domain of the semi-skilled. Again, in many firms there is a concentration on a very narrow range of highly specialized processes for which men could be trained in a comparatively short period if there were no collective agreements which prevent the use of other than fully-qualified men for these jobs.

How far such a redeployment of adult workers might alleviate the shortage cannot be estimated; and as this enquiry was concerned entirely with the recruitment and training of young workers, and not with the use made of them when fully qualified, no evidence is offered on this point. It is mentioned merely as a possible field for further investigation and negotiation. But insofar as the regulations covering the entry to skilled trades are concerned, the unions, with the exceptions already named, do not unduly restrict numbers of entrants.

Nor is the widely held view that boys do not wish to train for skilled work borne out by the evidence. It is often said that the piece work rates paid for semi-skilled jobs are so high that boys are lured away from the trades that require apprenticeship by the chances of easy money. That many boys *do* choose this semi-skilled work in preference to training is of course true; and it is well that it is so, for the amount of work for which a long training is needed is very much less in quantity than that for which semi-skilled workers suffice. Even if we include all jobs requiring as much as three years' training (and that is two years less than apprenticeship) the total is no more than a third of the jobs open to boys. But all the evidence shows that there is no lack of adequate numbers of boys eager to be accepted for training for these jobs; and in certain industries there is a long waiting list of applicants. This bears out indeed the results of earlier surveys on the factors which influence the choice of employment of school-leavers, which led to the conclusion that pay ranks well below the interest of the work itself and its future prospects, in the estimation of a large proportion of young workers faced with the choice of a job. It is only for a very few trades that the shortage of applicants is serious and those are mainly 'dirty trades' (iron foundries and the 'trowel' trades). Nor is the enthusiasm for the more interesting work shortlived, for broken apprenticeships are rare. And, again with the exception of the printing crafts, the large majority of apprentices claim and receive deferment of National Service and remain with their employers until their training is completed.

The main difficulty comes, in fact, not from the small supply of potential skilled workers but from the inadequate facilities for training them. The big deficiency shown in one industry after another included in this survey is in the supply of vacancies for which would-be apprentices can apply. For various reasons, differing to some extent in each industry investigated, there are large numbers of firms who employ skilled adults but who take no part in training them and who therefore rely on the pool of recruits trained by other firms. Many employers with good training schemes said during interviews that they had no objection to their young men seeking employment in other firms when they had completed their training; indeed many welcomed this as providing wider experience, but they felt that it did present them with a problem when it was a one-way traffic and their qualified apprentices went into firms which had not taken any share in the burden of training others who might come to them in exchange. The trouble comes from the fact that so many firms compete for the finished product but have no part in the responsibility for producing it.

Boy labour is no longer an asset to a firm, particularly on the short view, and this is the view that the small firm must inevitably take. The comparatively high wages, including the cost of a day off for classes, and the constant interruption to the work schedule when the apprentice is away taking his technical instruction, make the employment of apprentices a heavy burden to the establishment of modest size. Even though they are no longer 'tea and messenger boys' the amount produced by a young trainee is less than his cost for at least a couple of years, if not more, and it seems unlikely in consequence that the willingness of small firms to take apprentices will expand to any appreciable degree.

There have been a few tentative efforts to overcome this difficulty by a scheme in which a number of firms combine to train apprentices. In 1949 the Enfield and District Manufacturers' Association inaugurated a scheme incorporating 15 local firms, the basic idea of which was to provide full and comprehensive training for apprentices by giving them experience in other factories in the area, and thus offer a wider training than was available in any one establishment. The main objective of this scheme however was to train young men who might ultimately be suitable for executive posts, rather than to make it easier for the small firm to take on ordinary craft apprentices.[1] Three years later Unilever attempted a similar plan for some of its constituent establishments by setting up a Regional Apprenticeship Training Scheme in the North-West area. Working under a Regional Apprentice Training Manager the boys, who were carefully selected for a number of crafts—boilermakers, electricians, fitters, bricklayers, plumbers, etc.,—were given carefully graded instruction both theoretical and practical in the different establishments.[2] But this was a scheme established by one very large firm to use its own subsidiary companies in the training of its own apprentices. The most elaborate attempt to overcome the difficulties of the small or specialized firm is that begun in 1954 by the West London Group of the Engineering Industries' Association. As the aim of the participating firms was to avoid the expense incurred by each firm in giving time, thought and executive personnel to the

---

[1] B.A.C.I.E. Journal, July/August, 1940.
[2] *Ibid.* March/April, 1953.

supervision of apprentices, they invited a firm of industrial consultants, Industrial Administration (R. & A.) Ltd., to design and operate a scheme of Group Apprenticeship Training on behalf of them all.

In this scheme each firm accepts as many apprentices as it wishes and indentures them in the usual way. The initial selection is made by Industrial Administration Ltd. on the basis of an interview and a simple examination, though the final selection rests with the sponsoring firm which indentures them and which pays their wages. All the boys sponsored by the participating firms are formed into a group, which is controlled by a committee of representatives of member firms, the Youth Employment Service and educational organizations, with an officer of Industrial Administration Ltd. as its executive official. The cost of his services and of the administrative expenses is borne by the member firms in proportion to the number of apprentices they have in the scheme—a very much cheaper way of dealing with training than if each had to make separate provision. In the beginning each apprentice works with his own firm, but later will move about within the constituent firms in the group, so as to gain wide experience. The course of training followed is that agreed by the National Joint Body of the Engineering and Allied Employers' National Federation and the Confederation of Shipbuilding and Engineering Unions. At the end of the apprenticeship it is proposed to issue an Engineering Industries' Group Apprenticeship Certificate based on a series of practical tests.[1]

It took some time, naturally enough, to overcome some of the difficulties in so novel a scheme but, in the years since the inauguration of the venture, nine groups have come into operation with 136 member firms registered between them, employing altogether 190 apprentices. Five of these groups are in the Greater London area (of which the two oldest, West and North-West London, have between them 100 apprentices) and the remainder are in the Midlands. For convenience of administration groups are usually composed

[1] *Apprenticeship Training for Small Firms,* a report by the Engineering Industries' Association.

of between 12 and 20 firms providing for the training of 60–80 apprentices. But both the size of the groups and the number of apprentices depend on local conditions—particularly the travelling facilities available for the interchange of apprentices. The cost to the firm of being relieved of the responsibility for looking after its apprentices has been kept as low as possible. A fee of £5 is payable on registration by a participating firm and then, £3 10s. is payable monthly in respect of each apprentice.[1]

Participating firms find that one advantage of the scheme is that it has attracted a good type of boy. The managing director of one such firm said, 'Previously parents were not keen to send their boys to the small firm where training facilities were bound to be restricted. Now however parents realize that a small firm participating in this scheme can give their boys as good a training as he would receive in a big organization—where competition for apprenticeships is often intense.'[2]

That the difficulty of attracting apprentices to the small firm may still exist, however, is shown by the fact that in January, 1957, there were 50 vacancies for apprentices unfilled in all these groups together. This was probably due to their novelty, for some of the groups had only just been established.[3]

Although there is very little wastage of skilled workers during the period of apprenticeship it is possible that the leakage is much greater when men return from National Service. When they are called up efforts are made to allocate qualified men to duties which will enable them to make use of the skill they have acquired before joining the Services, but this is not always possible. Training and employment as soldiers must take precedence of everything else and there are limited possibilities in the Forces of using certain civilian skills. In a Conference on Industry and National Service held in Edinburgh in 1954 Brigadier F. G. A. Parsons, Deputy Director of Manpower Planning at the War Office, said 'The

[1] *Iron and Steel*, June, 1955.
[2] *Business*, Journal of Management, March, 1956.
[3] Correspondence with Industrial Administration (R. & A.) Ltd.

chief cause of discontent is the fact that we cannot train young men in the trades we want because the Army is not all tradesmen. It is a fighting Service. 42% of our National Service intake goes to the R.A.C., the Royal Artillery, and the Infantry, and these corps have fewer trades in them which are equivalent to civilian trades.'[1]

Experience varies greatly from one trade to another. It is easier, for example, for a motor mechanic or an electrical engineer to find work in the Forces that makes use of their knowledge and proficiency than it is for a compositor or a mosaic layer. It may happen therefore that a young man comes out of the Forces after his two years' service with quite different ideas of civilian employment than he had when he joined up. What is perhaps more important is that he is probably married or is contemplating getting married, so that he is more concerned with getting as high pay as he can than he was when he was apprenticed and thus, instead of returning to the skilled craft for which he trained, he turns off into semi-skilled work where he hopes by high piece rates and overtime to make enough to furnish a home. How much wastage of skilled men occurs after National Service it is impossible to say, for there are no records from which this information might be drawn, but it seems probable that it is considerable.

Some of the largest firms with well-equipped and well-staffed personnel departments make great efforts to keep in touch with the young men they have trained whilst they are serving; and when men are home-based and get frequent leave in their home town, this is not too difficult. In such cases there is a strong probability that the men will return to the firms that have trained them and to the work for which they trained. But only a minority of firms can afford the expense involved in this; and many firms expressed the view that a considerable number of trained men are lost not only to the individual firm, but to the industry as a whole, in consequence of the Service break.

The only detailed study from which some idea of the wastage can be gained has been made by J. Ferguson and

[1] *In Their Early Twenties*, T. Ferguson & J. Cunnison, p. 23.

J. Cunnison and published in 1956 in a book called *In Their Early Twenties*. This book follows an earlier study *The Young Wage Earner* made by the same authors and published in 1951. This gave an account of more than 1,300 boys who left school in Glasgow at the beginning of 1947, and detailed their health, industrial progress and leisure time interests over the following three years. By that time the boys were ready for National Service and in the second study the authors followed their careers in the Services and during the subsequent two years of employment. The group whose history is thus recorded is not strictly comparable with the apprentices who are the subject of the present study since the authors deliberately excluded from their later survey those boys in their original group who had deferred National Service in order to complete apprenticeship. There were indeed some apprentices in their group but they were those who had not asked for deferment and who were more likely therefore to be less settled in their trades, or on the whole to be doing less well in them. Whether this factor accounts for the wastage amongst them or not we cannot say, but the Survey shows that wastage did in fact take place and to a considerable extent. Of the 105 newly enlisted men who had been serving apprenticeship when they were called up only 60, that is 59%, were in skilled work still by the age of 22. This movement away from skill was not confined to boys of any particular rating of scholastic ability but was found at all levels though with perhaps some slight emphasis on those assessed as 'poor'.

But it is evidently not only the break of Service life which causes this drain from skill, for of the 58 boys serving apprenticeship at the age of 18 who had not asked for deferment but who were rejected as medically unfit and who could therefore have continued their training, only 37, that is, 64%, were actually employed in skilled work at the age of 22.

One cannot generalize too far from these figures. Both those accepted and those who in fact were ready to break their training but were rejected as unfit, were presumably the less stable trainees and less convinced of their desire to become skilled men. Moreover, and perhaps more important, these lads do not offer a representative section of that age group throughout the country. Glasgow suffered desperately between the two wars and most of these boys grew up in homes of grinding poverty and destitution. It is likely that these factors may also have exerted a lasting influence upon their estimation of the value of skilled work as a life career. But the figures do show a disquieting amount of loss of skill even though they do not provide any exact measurements of its quantity.

On the other hand the Services provide an additional source of skilled labour to those trained through civilian apprenticeship, for they offer training for young recruits which is accepted by the appropriate unions as entitling them to membership after demobilization. In Ferguson and Cunnison's Survey there were a small number—14 lads— whose experience during their two Service years counted towards their civilian apprenticeship and who were actually in skilled work by the time they were 22. But the more remarkable way in which the Services contribute to the supply of civilian skills is by their schemes of training for boys who enter well before the National Service age of call-up. All three Services offer opportunities of this type to suitable boys, between the ages of 15 and 17 as far as the Army and Navy are concerned, and between 15½ and 16½ for the R.A.F. The Army maintains three Apprentice Schools at which boys are given thorough training in one of a long list of crafts, after which, subject to reaching a certain standard of competence, they are eligible for skilled membership of the appropriate trade union on leaving the Service. The Navy has a similar establishment for the training of Artificer Apprentices, and the Air Force admits Aircraft Apprentices. In all three there is a qualifying examination as well as a medical examination before entry, so that only boys likely to be able to master the theoretical instruction, as well as the practical skill, are accepted; in return for this free education the boys have to agree to serve for a certain period after they reach the age of 18; in the case of the Army, for 8 years with the colours, and 4 in the Royal Army Reserve; in the Navy for 12 years and in the R.A.F. for 13 years. Men may elect to serve for various periods after completing this obligation and no doubt many do; but as a result of these schemes a flow of well-trained skilled men in a wide range of crafts goes from the Services into industry at about the age of 30 or thereabouts.

What addition this makes to the skilled labour force it is difficult to estimate; but there is no doubt that it is large enough to be significant. The Army Apprentice Schools have an annual output of trained men of about 650; the Royal Air Force admits between 1,000 to 1,250 apprentices a year, and the Royal Navy an average of 530. A considerable proportion of all of these sign on for an added period of service, but even so it is probable that about 1,500 to 2,000 highly qualified men move from the Services into civilian life each year.

V

FORMAL TECHNICAL EDUCATION

TECHNICAL Education has been a late starter in the educational system. Until the last century it was assumed that any necessary instruction required by those entering industry would be given to them by their masters during the period of apprenticeship. When new knowledge revolutionized industrial techniques England was far ahead of any competitor, and so generally prosperous that there seemed no reason to change this view. It continued to be taken for granted that any worker could learn on the job whatever he needed to know to make him an efficient producer. Indeed, the first attempts at providing any technical instruction for workers were not designed to make them more productive but were an expression of the anxiety of the liberal-minded in the nineteenth century to help the uneducated in self-improvement. The Mechanics' Institutes came into existence as a result of the contact made by Professor George Birkbeck, who held the Chair of Natural Philosophy in Glasgow, with artisans who under his direction were making apparatus that he required for his lectures. He was so struck by their intelligence and anxiety to learn, that he decided to start a course of lectures 'solely for persons engaged in the practical exercises of the mechanical arts, men whose situation in early life has precluded the possibility of acquiring even the smallest portion of scientific knowledge'.[1]

The lectures were extremely successful and were continued by his successor in the Chair when Birkbeck moved to London and began similar classes there; so that in 1823 the

[1] H. G. Barnard, *History of English Education*, p. 105.

groups of workers attending these courses were organized—both in London and in Glasgow—into Mechanics' Institutes. In the following years many smaller institutes were founded, principally in the industrial areas; but by the middle of the century their character had undergone profound changes. As there was not as yet any system of general education the number of manual workmen capable of understanding scientific principles was necessarily small, and the audiences of the Mechanics' Institute classes came to consist mainly of clerks and shopkeepers. These had little interest in technical instruction, and gradually the purpose for which the institutes had been founded receded into the background, and talks on matters of popular interest, or debates and social functions took the place of the technical instruction.

It was not until the second half of the nineteenth century that there arose any general concern about technical education, and this was primarily the result of the unwilling recognition that Britain's supremacy in world trade was beginning to be challenged by foreign competitors. The Great Exhibition in 1851, and those which followed in Paris in 1867 and 1878, provided evidence that this country was being rapidly overhauled by others, whose investments in the technical education of their workers were showing dividends in the rapid development of their industrial productive efficiency. A Commission appointed in 1870 under the chairmanship of the Duke of Devonshire issued a series of reports giving details of the steps that had been taken by other countries, and this led the Livery Companies of London, which for centuries had interested themselves in education, to found the City and Guilds of London Institute 'to provide and encourage education adapted to the requirements of all classes of persons engaged in or preparing to engage in manufacturing or other industries'. The Institute tried to carry out this function by providing financial grants to enable courses for artisans to be organized, and by holding examinations in technical subjects to provide standards of competence. It was under its auspices that there was opened in 1883 the Finsbury Technical College, which became the model on which technical colleges were established in other parts of the country. The interest aroused by these activities led to the appointment of the Royal Commission on Technical Instruction 1881–4, whose Report marks the first really important step in the provision of technical education as part of the public education system; for this Report not only recommended that Local Authorities should be empowered to establish secondary and technical schools and colleges but also insisted on the importance of a good general education as the essential basis for such technical instruction.

Two circumstances helped in the implementation of these recommendations. The first was the reorganization of local government in 1888 which brought into existence county and county borough councils with power to provide Rate Aid for education, and the second was that the Local Taxation (Customs and Excise) Act of 1890 made available to these new authorities certain funds (known from their origin as 'Whisky Money') which were used for the provision of technical education. Development was further helped by the Education Act, 1902, which laid the foundations for a coherent, integrated system of educational facilities which, whilst leaving much initiative in the hands of the local authorities, allowed the Board of Education guiding and supervisory functions over the whole field. Financial encouragement for the provision of classes in science and technology had previously come mainly from the Science and Art Department of the Department of Education, founded in 1883, which subsidized individual teachers or classes complying with the conditions laid down by the Department. Although the classes were mainly held in the evenings for the benefit of those employed in earning their living, some day schools had also been enabled to introduce these subjects into their curricula. But now the Board of Education began to give grants not for individual classes, but to enable schools to institute 'grouped courses' which might provide a sound basis of technical knowledge. Henceforward, therefore, from the beginning of the century grants were no longer confined to subjects approved by the Science and Art Department but were available for almost any branch of instruction, and there grew up the system of courses which has continued to develop up to the present: minor courses such as those in plastering or patternmaking, intended to provide instruction which is immediately applicable to the practice of a particular occupation—and major courses whose aim is to teach principles of general application to the whole of the operations of an industry. From these grew the technical colleges and junior technical schools on which have been founded the technical secondary schools of the present time.

As a result of these developments there came into existence two types of school, both of which had a predominantly technical bias. The first, which was almost entirely confined to London, was the trade school (though this name was not always employed), which aimed at preparing its pupils for a particular occupation such as building or furniture-making. The children entered at the age of 13+ for a two-year course, half of which consisted of general subjects and half of lessons and practice in the type of work to which the school was devoted. In the second type of junior technical school the aim was to provide an educational background for those who intended to go into some form of industrial work, without having first made up their minds which particular occupation they hoped to enter. Most of these schools drew up their curricula with entry into some form of engineering as the broad objective but they did not prepare their pupils for any one particular branch, much less for any specific craft, within the industry. They aimed at giving their pupils a general understanding of principles, together with intellectual discipline, and a training in the handling of tools which would enable them to apply what they had learnt to the work of the particular occupation they entered, when they began to earn. Neither of these types had developed at all extensively before the war. In 1938 the total provision covered no more than 31,248 pupils distributed as follows:

Technical and Trade Schools	20,551
Commercial Schools	7,350
Nautical Training Schools	867
Junior Art Departments	2,480

Of the 20,000 odd in technical and trade schools, over

15,000 were boys in schools preparing to enter some branch of engineering or building.[1]

In the reorganization of the educational system brought about by the Education Act, 1944, it was this second type of junior technical school that was favoured, and these became the basis of the secondary technical schools, one of the three branches of secondary provision (grammar, modern and technical) into which post-primary education is now divided. Following the aim of providing a sound general education for all young citizens up to the age of 15 the emphasis in these schools has moved from junior *technical* school to *secondary* technical school, i.e. they come within the orbit of secondary education which is compulsory for all young people between the ages of 11+ and 15, and the name simply designates the *type* of secondary education provided. They are intended for those whose interests lie primarily in the practical field, and whilst giving as broad an educational foundation as possible, stress the application of the work carried on to various groups of industries and occupations. The number of pupils in secondary technical schools remains surprisingly small, particularly for a country which is so highly industrialized and commercialized as this. Of the three types of secondary school, grammar, technical, and modern, the first contains 20% of primary school-leavers, the third takes 75%, and the technical only 5%.[2]

The main provision of technical education however has never been part of the basic system of educational facilities but has grown up in the field of 'Further Education' of which it forms the largest and most highly developed section; and this at once makes a clear distinction between its work and that of the secondary technical school. In the latter, education is carried on entirely during the day and is full-time; and the attendance of those registered as pupils is compulsory, at least until the legal school-leaving age has been reached. In the former, on the other hand, the majority of the classes are carried on outside working hours, usually in the evening (though there are similar day classes for those on late shifts)

[1] Ministry of Education Pamphlet No. 1, *The Nation's Schools*, p. 17, 1945.
[2] M.D. 9703 of 1956, *Technical Education*.

and most of the students attend only part-time. But the biggest distinction is that there is no statutory obligation on the part of any category of students to attend. The emphasis is laid on the word 'statutory', for now in a good many cases attendance at day classes is a condition of employment enforced by the employer. Already in the 'seventies certain pioneer firms such as Messrs. Mather and Platt and Messrs. Brunner, Mond, had established Works Schools for their own employees, and as time went on many others followed their example, or instead took advantage of the facilities provided by the State to release their young employees to attend classes during working hours without loss of pay. Both the Education Act, 1918, and that of 1944, envisaged the extension of this system to cover all those under 18 years of age whatever their occupation, not merely to enable them to have technical instruction but to continue their general education. Unfortunately neither the Continuation Schools designed by the earlier Act nor the County Colleges included in the latter one have actually materialized, and adolescent Day Release is almost entirely confined to those industries in which the employers believe that some technical education will be of advantage to young workers in learning their trade.

The main body of students attending technical institutions however is not there because they have been sent by their employers, but because they have chosen to give up some of their leisure time to equip themselves more satisfactorily for their work, and in age they range from 16 to almost anything. The types of classes provided for them by the technical colleges can be divided into two main categories—those intended to help train technicians (and to a smaller extent professional personnel) and those provided for the training of craftsmen. In the first group are courses, some of them attended by full-time students, which prepare for recognized professional qualifications of different levels (including in a few cases the degrees of the University of London) and for the National Certificates which were established in 1921 to provide recognized credentials for engineers working in industry and studying in the evening. In the second are courses, both theoretical and practical, designed to increase the skill and understanding of the boy apprenticed to a craft. Both types of course are faced with the same problem:

(i) how to ensure that the training given is, in fact, well adapted to the needs of those employed in particular occupations, and

(ii) how to maintain a good standard of accomplishment by the pupils which will be recognized and accepted by employing bodies, irrespective of the particular institution in which the instruction has been given.

One of the occupational diseases of all educational institutions is to suffer from a certain hardening of the arteries. Once courses have become well established along certain lines they tend to stiffen into an unchanging stereotyped pattern. Such rigidity is always harmful whatever the subject of study, but it is particularly so when the instruction is intended to have direct application to industrial work. The rate of technological change has been extremely rapid in the present century and there would be little profit to be gained for industry if the content of the courses in technical education failed to keep pace with these changes. Very close contact is therefore necessary between the educational institutions and the industries for which students are trained. An attempt to maintain and develop this intimate relationship is made partly by the existence of representative Boards of Governors attached to particular institutions, and partly by Regional Advisory Councils which can bring their influence to bear on a whole locality. Although it is by no means universal, a large and growing number of technical colleges are assisted by Boards of Governors whose members are drawn from the leading industries with which the institution is particularly concerned, as well as from the Ministry of Education, the Local Education Authority and the institution itself, and in this way the interrelatedness of the instruction given in the college and the technological changes in industry can be kept constantly under review.

Usually, however, in an industrial area there is more than one technical institution and there are problems which are common to them all, whilst they differ materially from those of other areas whose chief occupations are in a different field.

It was the realization of the diversity that exists in regional industrial developments which led Lord Eustace Percy, when he was President of the Board of Education, to advocate the establishment of Regional Councils on which industrialist and educator could discuss their common problems from their different angles. With Mr. A. Abbot, then Chief Inspector of Technical Education, he arranged for a survey of technical education in Yorkshire to be undertaken in 1925-6, and from this resulted the foundation of the Yorkshire Council for Further Education which, by organizing industrial advisory committees on which employers, operatives and the institutions could discuss together the needs of the locality, has had a marked influence on technical education in that county.

Between that date and the outbreak of war further similar surveys were made and led to the establishment of other local advisory councils in South Wales, the Midlands, and the Manchester district.[1] In this field, as in so many, the war acted as a forcing house and immediately after the passing of the Education Act, 1944, a Select Committee, set up under the chairmanship of Lord Eustace Percy to consider higher technical education, recommended, among other matters, the setting up of a network of Regional Advisory Councils to cover the whole of the country. This advice was at once accepted by the Ministry of Education which has since organized the Councils, composed of representatives of Local Education Authorities, universities, industry, commerce and the technical institutions. They work through standing sub-committees which are related to particular industries and interests. At the apex of the Advisory Council system is the National Advisory Council for Education in Industry and Commerce established in 1947 to co-ordinate the activities of the local bodies.

The essential job of the Regional Advisory Councils is to equate the local provision of technical education to the regional needs of industry and commerce, and to formulate recommendations to make good any deficiencies which they find. But their value, as that of any other piece of political

[1] P. F. R. Venables, *Technical Education*, Chapter 5.

machinery, depends on the seriousness with which the members take their duties and opportunities, and on the readiness of those whose interests they represent to bring to their notice difficulties that might possibly be easily overcome if the institutions were aware of them. Many employers, for example, justify their unwillingness to allow the Day Release of their young workers on the grounds that there are no suitable classes available within a reasonable distance, without bothering to consult their representatives on the Advisory Councils to see whether this is a situation that cannot be altered. But, at their best, the Councils, whilst unable to compel any change, since their function is entirely advisory, can ensure that the rapidly changing technological needs of industry are kept continually in mind when courses of instruction are being planned.

It is however in the answer to the second problem—that of providing generally accepted standards of competence—that a much more direct and powerful influence is exercised over the work of the technical colleges. Mention has already been made of the City and Guilds of London Institute which, by its grants to those providing technical instruction of a type to win its approval, was amongst the earliest to stimulate this work. The Institute was founded in 1877 after a meeting of the Livery Companies of London at the Mansion House at which the following resolution was adopted:

'That it is desirable that the attention of the Livery Companies be directed to the promotion of Education not only in the Metropolis but throughout the country, and especially to Technical Education with the view of educating young artisans and others in the scientific and artistic branches of their trade.'[1]

In addition to providing subsidies for classes and teachers it decided to conduct examinations of their pupils to ensure that good standards were maintained, and the certificates gained by those who pass these examinations are now universally recognized credentials of different levels of competence in technical subjects. When it is thought that

[1] *Ibid.*, p. 150.

examinations should be instituted in a new subject, a committee of all the interests concerned is set up—industry, the technical colleges, the government departments and professional institutions, and, if the initial investigation seems to justify the inclusion of the subject in the examinations, a permanent advisory committee is established which drafts the syllabus and regulations for the courses which the technical colleges are to supply.

The City and Guilds of London Institute is not the oldest of the examining bodies. The originator of this system is the Union of Lancashire and Cheshire Institutes which stems directly from the Mechanics' Institutes of the early nineteenth century. Founded in 1839, it began to hold its examinations in 1847 and has continued to the present time. It was followed half a century later by the Union of Educational Institutions which began to perform a similar service for the Southern Counties, and this, in its turn, was followed by the East Midland Educational Union established in 1911, and the Northern Counties Technical Examination Council founded in 1920. All these unions are now partnerships of Local Education Authorities and educational institutions and with the help of the Advisory Committees representative of all the interests concerned, they draft syllabuses and hold examinations in technical, commercial and literary subjects.

The examinations of the City and Guilds are held for three different levels:

(1) Intermediate: represents an adequate attainment in a craft or trade and subjects which are basic to it, e.g. the level usually required of the higher grade of industrial workers who have acquired a skill in a fairly strictly defined operation but who have not been required to serve an apprenticeship.

(2) Final: represents complete competence for all normal purposes in the selected craft or trade and the steps basic to it, i.e. the level required of skilled craftsmen, mechanics and artisans who have served a fully recognized apprenticeship.

(3) Full Technological Certificate: represents a wide field of attainment and competence, indicating that the holder has a comprehensive knowledge of his subject and its place in the industry. Given the right qualities of personality and

character this should qualify the holder to become a departmental head or works manager.

Any student over the age of 15/16 can enter for these examinations, and there are no regulations which lay down any definite prior education attainments on the part of the entrants. The four Examining Unions work in close co-operation with the City and Guilds and hold examinations of a similar type at the Intermediate stage; but students who are successful in these proceed to the Final examination of the City and Guilds of London Institute.

Both the Examining Unions and the City and Guilds Institute were originally concerned almost exclusively with the lower ranges of industrial work, and until 1921 there were no available qualifications to act as incentives to part-time education for those in higher grades. In that year the Board of Education (as it then was), after discussion with the Institution of Mechanical Engineers, decided to establish a qualification for engineers working in industry and undertaking part-time study. Thus there came into existence the National Certificate scheme, first in Mechanical Engineering, and later in a large number of other branches of work—Civil, Electrical and Production Engineering, Building, Metallurgy, etc.

The National Certificates which are awarded by the Ministry of Education in conjunction with the appropriate professional organization are of two levels:

(1) Ordinary National Certificates are awarded for the successful completion of a systematic part-time group course, usually of three years' duration, adapted to the needs of students admitted at the age of approximately 16 years and who have qualified for admission to the course by continued full-time education up to the age of 16, or by previous attendance (usually for 2 years) at suitable part-time preliminary courses.

(2) Higher National Certificates are awarded for the successful completion of advanced part-time courses usually of two years' duration, designed for students who have obtained the Ordinary National Certificates or who have otherwise reached a similar standard of attainment (e.g. the

General Certificate of Education at Advanced Level). These advanced courses aim at reaching the standard of university degree work in the subjects taken.

The National Certificates are usually accepted by professional bodies as exempting candidates from part of the qualifications of those wishing to be admitted as members, and thus provide an alternative route to professional status for those who for some reason have not been able to go to a university. Some technical colleges go further than this and offer full-time courses of study which enable those following them to sit for the degrees of the University of London. Much of the work of the technical colleges is devoted to courses of this type, which in general are far above the standard set for craft apprentices and consequently have little direct connection with the main subject of this enquiry. They are mentioned only to give an outline sketch of the institutions in which apprentices may get their formal instruction and because it is theoretically possible, though in practice very rarely accomplished, for an adolescent craft apprentice to advance to these higher courses.

Although the County Colleges envisaged in the Education Act, 1944, have not been set up, the effort made to get this scheme included in the reorganization of the educational system has not been entirely wasted, for it has had a marked influence on the training of apprentices. Before the war there were only a few firms that maintained their own Works Schools or that sent their young employees to classes at local technical institutions, but in the post-war period, and largely as a result of the insistence that the adolescent must continue his education at least part-time, if he is to develop whatever potentialities he possesses, there has been a remarkable growth in both these particulars. It is still, of course, only the largest firms, or those whose directors are most actively convinced of the value of formal teaching, that run their own Works Schools as a normal regular part of their organization. Those that do, follow very much the same pattern. The School provides first an induction course, i.e. it helps the new recruit to bridge the gap between school and industry by explaining the various branches of the work, the types of product for which the firm is responsible, and the general processes which contribute to them. Secondly, it often takes charge of the pre-apprenticeship period of from six to twelve months' duration in which the new boy is tried out on various types of work before being entered at the age of 16 as an apprentice to the particular craft of his (and the firm's) choice. Thirdly, it keeps a generally watchful eye on the work done by the apprentice at the technical college, or it may supplement this by teaching in particular fields. But for the most part, Works Schools do not provide the formal technical instruction which enables apprentices to take the examinations described above, though there are a number of instances in which the technical school is actually on the works premises, using a building and equipment provided by the firm and co-operating with a Local Education Authority which is responsible for the actual instruction.

But it is in the second respect—the Day Release of apprentices—that the most profound change is taking place. Before the war the number of firms willing to release their workers was comparatively small, though a much larger number gave evidence of their belief that something more than practice in the shops was required to teach a boy a craft by making it a condition of apprenticeship that he should attend technical classes for a certain number of evenings a week. Very valuable work was often done in this way but it was only a minority of boys that drew real benefit from it. It was asking a great deal of young people to give up their leisure after a long and exacting day's work, particularly as the technical school might be a long distance away; and for an apprentice getting a very low wage the expense of travel, as well as the time taken, was a serious drawback.

But in the new apprenticeship schemes which have been agreed since the war great emphasis is laid on the requirement to release workers during working hours without loss of pay to attend technical classes. By the provisions of most of these schemes apprentices should be released from the beginning of their apprenticeship period until they reach their 18th birthday, for one full day or two half days per week over a 30-week year, but as has been mentioned in Chapter

IV, one industry, printing, extends this to cover the whole term of training up to 21. It is no wonder therefore that the number of pupils in part-time technical classes in the 16 to 17 age groups has increased so remarkably since the end of the war. In 1939 there were only 41,000 such students; there are now well over a quarter of a million. What proportion of the total of apprentices this figure represents it is, unfortunately, impossible to say, for there are no relevant statistics. In the White Paper on Technical Education[1] figures are given in which, unhappily, it is not possible to have complete confidence. In the engineering, shipbuilding and electrical goods group of industries, for example, it is stated that 90% of the number of those under 18 are released for part-time education. One would, of course, expect that this group, which contains the highest proportion of skilled workers of any large industry, would have a large number of young workers serving apprenticeship; but it would be surprising to find such a high proportion as 90% in this category and still more surprising if all of them were released to attend classes. In fact the proportion of young workers undergoing apprenticeship is far below this figure of 90%. Of the young men in this group who registered for National Service in 1955 at the age of 18 only 78% were receiving training lasting at least three years, and as an apprenticeship lasts five years it follows that a smaller proportion than this were apprentices. From the evidence given in Chapter IV showing the scarcity of apprentices among several categories of firms in this group, it seems likely that the percentage is quite considerably smaller.

As the County Colleges have not been set up there is no statutory obligation to release adolescents for instruction, and the only agreements made are confined to those undergoing a five-year apprenticeship. At the best therefore, even if all employers honoured the agreement, and if educational facilities were available in every area, the percentage of boys being released would necessarily be considerably below 78% and not 90%. In fact, however, as will be shown later, not all employers do release their workers, and not every area is able to provide the necessary facilities.

[1] Cmd. 9703, 1956.

In the building industry 45% of the total number of boys attached to the industry are recorded in the White Paper as released for instruction; but here again, according to the National Registration figures, only 59% were having training lasting at least three years. As has been shown in the account of this industry in Chapter IV a great many firms find particular difficulty in employing apprentices and a very large number of skilled men have infiltrated into the craftsmen's ranks by other means. It is almost certain therefore that this figure, too, is too optimistic.

But whilst it is probable that the totals are overestimated, the information given is valuable as showing the wide divergence between areas and between different industries. In Scotland as a whole the percentage of Day Release falls far below that in England and Wales. The Scottish statistics give boys and girls together as one group and this is likely to lower the average as few girls train for skilled crafts; but the figure of 20% recorded for day classes in building and contracting in Scotland can be compared with the 45% in England and Wales, as this industry has predominantly male employment. In engineering, metal manufacture and vehicles the Scottish proportion is only 10%—in printing only 3%.

For the industries included in this Survey the figures given in the White Paper are as follows:

Boys under 18 released for Day Classes as a percentage of the numbers insured

	England and Wales		Scotland
Engineering, Shipbuilding and Electrical Goods	90	Engineering, Metal Manufacture and Vehicles [1]	16
Building and Contracting	45		20
Paper and Printing	33		3

Even though these figures have almost certainly been considerably overestimated the relationship between them is interesting.

[1] The motor vehicle repairing industry is not given separately here as it is included in the vehicle building industry in the official statistics.

In the enquiry firms were asked to state the number of their apprentices who were attending Day Release classes at that time, and in the following summary these figures have been related to the firms which employ apprentices. Those that have no apprentices on their books are omitted from the percentage calculations.

In general engineering it is evidently the small firm that finds Day Release difficult, for just over one-third of those with less than 100 employees allowed no Day Release whereas the scheme was operating in the large majority of bigger establishments. In electrical engineering, on the other hand, only one firm—and that a medium-sized firm—had no apprentices on Day Release, and in the iron and steel industry there were only two firms employing between 100 and 500 and two employing between 500 and 1,000 workers, in the same position. In iron foundries, however, the majority of small firms had no Day Release though all the large ones had. In shipbuilding the majority of the firms released, at least, some of their workers, but this industry is unique in that some of its largest employers had no Day Release at all and one with over 600 apprentices was in this group.

In the building industry three-quarters of the small firms (under 50 workers) allowed Day Release, and the same was true of the large majority of the medium-sized firms which bear the main burden of apprenticeship. In printing again most firms released their apprentices, though here there were marked divergences between small and large establishments; only one of the large firms had no Day Release, whilst this was true of about one-quarter of the smallest. The motor vehicle repairing industry showed an unusually high proportion of Day Release amongst the small firms—with well over three-quarters of those having apprentices allowing them to go to day classes.

Not too much reliance must be placed on these percentages, for the question was not always answered even by firms who had filled in all the rest of the questionnaire; and it is probable that a larger proportion of those who do permit Day Release replied than of those who do not. But whilst the considerable number of firms in which Day Release is found is evidence of a growing appreciation on the part of industry of the importance of provision for technical instruction, there are still many employers, even in the industries with a large body of skilled workers, who are not convinced of its value and who seize any opportunity that offers itself to evade carrying out this part of the apprenticeship agreements.

Full employment has both stimulated and discouraged the expansion of Day Release. The shortage of young workers which is the direct consequence of the low birth-rate just before the war, coupled with booming post-war industry, has put young people at such a premium that there is intense competition between industries as a whole and between individual firms to attract young people to them. Employers vie with one another in their offer of amenities and extras that might weight the scale in their favour—free luncheon vouchers, no Saturday work, *Music While You Work*, welfare provisions, etc., are widely advertised; and in districts where there are many competitors for the type of boy likely to go into skilled work, the promise of Day Release is often one of the offers held out by anxious employers, even by those who themselves are contemptuous of the value of formal instruction.

On the other hand, the shortage has pushed up the wages of adolescent workers more than those of adults. The percentage increase in the average weekly earnings of youths in 1956 over those of 1938 was 285 as compared with 241 for adult men; or, if only the post-war period is taken into account, boys' earnings have increased by 110% since 1947 in comparison with a 91% increase for men. This means that the payment of a day's wage without any compensating output is a consideration which the employer must take seriously into account, and which, for those who take a short-term view, or who remain unconvinced that attendance at classes is worth while, seems an unnecessarily heavy burden to bear. In most of the industries with which this enquiry is concerned, however, profits have been so high that it is not the financial consideration which weighs most heavily with the average firm; it is rather the actual loss of the productive work which they are unwilling to forgo. In his first year the apprentice does not make much contribution to the firm's output, but as he gets more familiar with the processes he becomes a more and more valuable asset, so that even many of the firms that allow Day Release watch impatiently for the apprentice's eighteenth birthday when they can be free of this obligation. So much so, in fact, that many ruthlessly withdraw their apprentices on the very day they reach this age, irrespective of the fact that they may, perhaps, be preparing to take a qualifying examination only two or three weeks later—a procedure which is not only extremely discouraging both to the technical college and to the apprentice, but which gives a truer idea than any number of lip-service protestations of the attitude of the employer to the value of class teaching.

At the same time it must be admitted that the release of young workers may put firms into much greater difficulties than simply the loss of the potential day's output of the apprentice himself, and this is particularly so where the productive unit is comparatively small. Even though the technical colleges recognize that many of the courses must be repeated throughout the week, so as to allow boys to fit in with the requirements of their productive work, some definite time-tabling is essential. The number able to attend at a certain time must be sufficient to make it worthwhile for the college to use staff and equipment and this means that employers must be prepared to release the pupils at a specified time and on specified days. If the firm is large enough to employ a considerable number of apprentices, suitable arrangements can be made, but for the small firms with only one or two boys at that particular stage the absence of the apprentices may seriously hinder the work of a group of adults. The employer who is truly convinced of the value of class-room instruction is prepared to make the sacrifice entailed; but it is part of the traditional outlook of industrialists in this country to be scornful of 'book knowledge' in the practical field, and those who share this attitude are naturally less willing to put themselves out for what, in their heart of hearts, they think to be unnecessary 'flim-flam'. With increased specialization there are many firms whose work has not the range which enables their apprentices to get a comprehensive training, and the college instruction is their only opportunity of learning processes outside the work of the particular firm. Without this training the apprentice, even when he has finished his time, is not qualified to move on to other firms with a different or a wider range of work. But to many employers it seems that they get little return for the bother they are put to if the apprentices are learning types of work which they will never ask them to do. If the theoretical instruction helps the apprentice to learn more quickly and more successfully to do the jobs required of him in the workshops in the remainder of the week, there is an obvious benefit to be put on the credit side, but when the returns are the less easily estimated long-term ones of creating a fully-qualified skilled labour force for the industry, the employer without the necessary vision and understanding sees no reason why he should put himself out and pay wages for something which is of so little direct benefit to himself. There are therefore many firms that feel that they discharge their obligations under the apprenticeship schemes if they permit boys who ask for Day Release to have it instead of insisting upon it for all, or they attach to it certain conditions, e.g. that the boy should also voluntarily attend one or two evening classes in addition to the classes given during his Day Release (this is, indeed, an integral part of the scheme for the building industry), or that one who fails to reach a certain standard in the course should have to repeat it in the evening at his own expense before being permitted to continue the day-time instruction.

At first sight this conditional permission might seem a good way of ensuring that young workers do not take their privileges too much for granted; but in fact it destroys the whole purpose of the scheme. The general tendency of modern trade unionism has been towards the demand for a shorter working day, both on the grounds of the great nervous strain imposed by modern industry and on those of the importance of adequate leisure to enable the worker to make up, by the wider contacts and interests of his outside life, for the ever narrowing specialization of his productive work. To insist on evening study for young workers is to go completely contrary to this trend and to impose an added burden at a time when it is most difficult to bear. The transition from school to industry is, in any event, an adjustment which imposes great strain on the adolescent. To take away from his decreased leisure time a couple of evenings a week for compulsory study is to add greatly to the rigours of this period.

It must not be thought however that employers and workers are at loggerheads on the evaluation of technical instruction; a great many of the apprentices also feel that it is wasting time to go back to school and that they could learn all that they need on the job. It is perhaps because of the large number in this category that employers feel that they are justified in separating the sheep from the goats by allowing time off only to those who give evidence of understanding the value of the instruction by sacrificing their own free time to add to it. Many boys, particularly those who find theoretical work specially trying, look forward eagerly to the end of their school days, when they hope that they will put all such troubles behind them for ever, and bitterly resent attendance at courses which they cannot easily master. The practical training given in the colleges is usually much enjoyed but the theoretical work for such boys as these is simply something to be endured.

In some cases the works are situated too far from any technical school for attendance to be possible. One firm wrote, 'Facilities for learning the theoretical side of engineering are unavailable. Evening classes in this town are elementary and to obtain the advanced teaching apprentices have to attend classes in Newcastle—unfortunately a total of two hours travelling by 'bus. We impress upon our boys the necessity of attending classes, but with little response. Actually, I cannot blame them—after working well during the day boys do not, as a rule, favourably consider putting in another five hours in the evening, and that is what going to classes in Newcastle involves.' In this particular instance the firm did not explain why it did not send its boys to day classes but it may have meant to infer that two hours' travelling to reach the class would mean too long a day for most of their young apprentices.

A large firm of builders, most of whose apprentices were

attending classes, wrote, 'Painter apprentices have been unable to find suitable classes in the locality.' Another firm in the motor vehicle repairing industry said, 'The nearest classes are 26 miles away.'

For those who do attend the Day Release classes, what is the result? Are the expense and the inconvenience to the firm justified? One of the difficulties with which the colleges have to contend in providing these courses is that there is practically no selection process for those accepted for apprenticeship and therefore for those released for the classes. A very few large firms with outstanding reputations can pick and choose from amongst those anxious to get into them, but the large majority are not in this position. A boy with a reasonably good school record from the point of view of character and not obviously medically unfit, usually stands as good a chance as any other. The probationary year between school-leaving age and 16, when he can begin his formal apprenticeship, gives the employer some opportunity to discover whether he is a decent biddable boy with some capacity to learn how to handle tools and so on, but it gives no indication of his intellectual gifts or interests. Where the attendance at courses is voluntary the classes are self-selective; those without interest don't begin and those unable to understand don't usually continue, but the technical colleges are in the position of having to deal with the whole mass of apprentices sent to them, whether the boys are interested in the theoretical work or not, and whether they are capable of learning or not. In many instances there can be no doubt that the boy's body is present when his mind is far away, until the moment comes for the practical work in which he feels he can really take part.

The difficulties experienced by apprentices in coping with the theoretical part of the instruction figured so largely in interviews with the staff of technical colleges that it was felt worth while to try to get some estimate of the numbers who reach the standard of a recognized credential. The courses of study attended by craft apprentices are designed to allow them to sit for the Intermediate City and Guilds examination set in their own subject at the end of three years, with the possibility of proceeding to the Final Certificate at the end of the five years' term.

It will be remembered (see p. 148) that the Intermediate Level is intended to show an adequate attainment in a craft, by workers who have acquired a skill in a fairly strictly defined operation, but have not been required to serve an apprenticeship, whilst the Final Certificate represents the level required of skilled craftsmen who have served a fully recognized apprenticeship. How many of this large number of apprentices attending the technical colleges actually achieve these levels? Unfortunately there are no records which provide an authoritative answer.

The City and Guilds Institute annually publishes its records of the number sitting for each examination and the results, but gives no indication (naturally enough) of the number of years of preparation taken, nor of whether the candidate is having a second attempt. The instructors in the colleges do not recommend a boy to sit for the examination unless there is a reasonable chance that he will pass; and if he fails he is often urged by the college to repeat the course (either day or evening) and try again.

As the examination candidates are thus carefully selected one could expect a reasonably good proportion of passes, and the average is, indeed, somewhere between 60 and 65%. But there are no records which show the number of boys who take the courses but who do not get as far as sitting for the examination.

As there is as yet no statutory obligation on boys under 18 to attend day classes the responsibility of ensuring attendance rests with the employers, so that if a boy drops out of the course, the college does not necessarily make enquiries. Some colleges try to keep track of those who do not attend by sending a card to the firm notifying non-attendance (this is in case the boy goes off on his own ploys when the firm thinks he is in class) and later if the absence continues, it asks if he has been withdrawn. But technical colleges, like most educational institutions, have only a small clerical staff and it is not possible in most cases for anything more to be done. Practically all those responsible for teaching apprentices were fairly certain in their own minds that a considerable proportion failed to reach the standard that would justify the recommendation to sit for the Intermediate City and Guilds examination, but they had no definite knowledge.

For this reason it was decided to undertake the task of tracing the history of groups of apprentices from the beginning of their technical instruction until they left the college. A number of colleges in the Home Counties and East Anglia agreed to co-operate by allowing a search of their registers to be made for this purpose. In each case the intake of craft apprentices to a craft course several years ago was taken, and the fortune of each individual throughout the ensuing years was traced and recorded. The results, it must be admitted, are rather startling, and seemed to be as much so to the colleges as to the investigator.

The majority of colleges follow the same procedure. A boy is admitted to the course during the first year of his apprenticeship, and it is expected that he will proceed through the three years' course that is planned to enable him to sit the Intermediate level of City and Guilds at the end of his third year. It is hoped that he will then continue with evening classes so as to reach Finals level by the end of his apprenticeship. As has been mentioned, only a minority actually sit this examination, for the college does not recommend a pupil to apply unless it thinks he has a sporting chance of success. But the college also has its own tests taken at the end of each year, which enable the instructors to see if the boy has reached a level from which he can profit from the next year's work. If he does not reach this standard he remains to repeat the course again in the hope that he may improve enough to pass after a second try. Only one of the colleges that figure in these records allows a boy to proceed to the next year's work, even though he has failed to reach the standard set by the college in his preceding year.

There is, naturally, some wastage from one year to another. Some boys leave the district and may perhaps attend classes elsewhere but disappear from these records. Some get discouraged and withdraw—where their employers permit it— or are withdrawn by their employers because of their failure.

Some reappear in the registers of evening classes and try to continue their studies in that way, but a certain proportion just vanish completely from the records. Some firms allow their apprentices to attend day classes throughout the five years of their apprenticeship, but these form a small minority. For the most part, those who do manage to pass Intermediate City and Guilds are expected, if they wish to proceed to Final City and Guilds, to do so by attending evening classes.

The following records are grouped in relation to the subject of the course the apprentice attended; and it must be understood that College A or B is not necessarily the same institution in each group.

MACHINE SHOP ENGINEERING

College A.

1953/4. Initial intake: 56 apprentices.

Of these 22 failed to satisfy the college test at the end of the first year and had to repeat it; 14 of these still failed to reach the standard by the end of the second year. The others passed and went on to the second year course. Of the original 56 only 3 managed to pass Intermediate City and Guilds.

The following table of the size of classes in this college taking first, second, and third year courses, shows how large a number failed to be able to proceed. It should be noted that many of those registered in any of these courses are repeating work because they failed the test set at the end of the preceding session.

Year	First year	Second year	Third year
1950/1	20	12	10
1951/2	29	23	9
1952/3	35	32	12
1953/4	63	46	13
1954/5	55	39	25
1955/6	70	52	29
1956/7	66	60	20

College B.

1950/1. Initial intake: 43.

Of these 19 failed to pass the first year test and had to repeat it. 4 eventually passed Intermediate City and Guilds, all of them at the second try.

1951/2. Initial intake: 26.

Of these 4 eventually passed Intermediate City and Guilds, of whom 2 went on to try for the Final City and Guilds, but failed.

College C.

This college is in rather a different position from those already mentioned. It intends to specialize entirely on more advanced work and was in process of transforming itself when it agreed to co-operate in the investigation. It had already discontinued its first-year course for apprentices, so that all of those in the initial intake had already completed the first year of the course at another institute and were able to be put at once into the second year of the course. These pupils had therefore already undergone a process of selection, and the results are seen in the rather larger number of successes in the following record:

1952/3. Intake: 49.

Of these, 17 failed to pass the test at the end of the year and had to repeat the course, and 5 left or were transferred to other colleges. Of the whole group eventually 17 passed Intermediate City and Guilds (15 requiring two tries to do it) and 5 went on to pass the Final City and Guilds.

1953/4. Intake: 67.

Of these 29 failed the end of session test and had to repeat the year. Eventually 25 of the whole group passed Intermediate City and Guilds (24 at the second try).

ELECTRICAL INSTALLATIONS

College A

The following table gives the numbers who registered for

courses in the various years and those who, by the end of 1956, had passed Intermediate City and Guilds.

Year	Initial intake	Passed City and Guilds
1950/1	44	5
1951/2	32	1
1952/3	35	3
1953/4	44	3

Many of those listed as the initial intake were repeating the course because they had been left behind the preceding year. Of the 1953/4 group, for example, 16 of the 44 passed the college test and moved on to the next year of the course; 28 failed and of those only 14 actually repeated the course (the others left); 5 of those 14 got through the first-year course at the second try but only two of them managed to pass the second-year course successfully.

College B

This college has no first-year courses so the boys admitted have already completed the first year of their work.

1952/3.

Of the 30 boys accepted for the second-year course, 22 failed to pass the college test at the end of the session and eventually only 5 of the original group passed Intermediate City and Guilds, all of them at the second try.

1953/4.

31 boys were admitted to the second-year course. At the end of the year 10 left or went to the Forces, 11 failed the college test and 10 went on to the third year of the course.

MOTOR VEHICLE WORK

College A

The following table gives the numbers who passed Intermediate City and Guilds by 1956 in relation to the number who were doing the first-year course in different years:

Year	Intake	Passed Inter. City and Guilds
1950/1	21	5
1951/2	30	5
1952/3	27	4
1953/4	38	1

The last line is significant as showing how rare it is for a boy to reach the prescribed standard in the three years of the course. Two or three more of this group will probably pass eventually but only after repeated tries. Of this group, for example, 17 failed to pass the first-year and 3 were repeating it still at the end of 1956.

College B

Initial intake: 33.

This group showed much better results than in most courses. 30 passed the first-year test and went on to the second-year course. 18 passed this and proceeded to the third year and 12 gained Intermediate City and Guilds.

College C

46 passed into the second-year course, of whom eventually 15 passed Intermediate City and Guilds, many at the second try.

CARPENTRY AND JOINERY

College A

1953/4. Initial intake: 51.

Of this group 36 passed the first-year test but 10 of these failed the second-year test and 9 eventually passed the Intermediate City and Guilds.

College B

1953/4. Initial intake: 14.

Of these 5 have passed Intermediate City and Guilds.

College C

This college differs from the others in that it is entirely devoted to technical instruction relating to the building industry. The following table gives the numbers who passed Intermediate City and Guilds by the end of 1956 and those beginning the course (or repeating the first year in the years stated).

Year	Initial intake	Passed Inter. City and Guilds
1950/1	52	18
1951/2	53	14
1952/3	57	22
1953/4	34	14

This series is noteworthy, for 10 of the 1952/3 group have passed the Final City and Guilds examination.

BRICKLAYING

College A

Year	Initial intake	Passed Inter. City and Guilds	Passed Final City and Guilds
1950/1	35	11	5
1953/4	56	13	–

Although 13 of this second group reached the Intermediate City and Guilds standard, 20 failed to pass the first-year test and 8 failed again after a further year's work and second try.

College B

This is again the college which specializes in Building Instruction.

Year	Initial intake	Passed Inter. City and Guilds	Passed Final City and Guilds
1950/1	15	5	4
1951/2	12	3	2 sat but failed
1952/3	14	5	5
1953/4	13	1	–

LETTERPRESS MACHINE PRINTING
1950/1.

The initial intake was 116 of whom all but 11 passed the first year. At this college there is no system of repeating a course in which one has been unsuccessful, and even those who fail to pass the test go on to the next year's work. Although so large a proportion passed the college test, the standard presumably could not have been very high for only 35 eventually sat the Intermediate City and Guilds examination, of whom 34 passed.

HAND COMPOSITION
1950/1

106 began the course, of whom 16 ultimately passed Intermediate City and Guilds.

LITHOGRAPHY
1950/1

54 began the course, of whom 8 were finally successful in Intermediate City and Guilds.

These last three records are all taken from the same College which specializes in technical instruction related to the printing industry. Its courses for craft apprentices are designed to cover five years and those who complete the whole term and reach the prescribed standard are given the College's own Certificate. In these groups, 20 of those in the Hand Composition course got the Five Year Course Certificate (9 of these had already passed Intermediate City and Guilds) and in the Lithography Course 6 received the College Certificate.

It must be emphasized that these are not exceptionally bad results chosen from a larger number. On the contrary, these are all the registers examined, chosen at random from all those relating to craft apprentice courses at the colleges which permitted an examination of their records. There was so little variation in the results of the analyses that there seemed to be little to be gained by adding to their number. In all these courses the number of apprentices who reach Final Level of the City and Guilds is so tiny as to be negligible, though this is supposed to be the standard required of a man who has served a full apprenticeship, and even the much lower Intermediate level, designed simply to show competence in a narrow range of operations by those who have not been apprenticed, is reached by only a very small minority. Moreover a very large number, far from getting any recognized credential, do not pass even the annual college tests.

Three possible explanations suggest themselves as having some bearing on these disastrously poor results. First, is the teaching competent? Second, are the boys sufficiently well-grounded in general education to be able to understand the technical instruction they are given? Third, are the examining bodies setting too high a standard for what can reasonably be expected of these apprentices?

To none of these questions can an authoritative answer be given, but from a great many discussions with industry, technical colleges and other interested bodies, certain impressions can be gained.

To be highly skilled in doing a job is one thing: to be able to teach somebody else to do it is quite another. This is particularly true when the job is a skilled manual operation because there is nothing in the work itself which trains one in verbal expression. A student of history, for example, is not necessarily a good teacher, but at least the medium he employs for his own analysis and research is words, and it is words in which he must express his ideas clearly and comprehensibly to his pupils. But very highly skilled manual workers are generally unused to expressing themselves verbally, and cannot easily explain to a class in an intelligent way what they are doing and, much less, why they are doing it. There is, of course, much more to good teaching than this; one must have some sympathy with the young and be able to look at a problem from their point of view so as to see where a difficulty may arise. But words are the essential medium, and without the gift, or trained capacity, to use words in a simple, telling and interesting manner, no amount of sympathetic understanding will make a good teacher.

The technical colleges therefore have a very serious staffing problem—their instructors must be highly skilled craftsmen with a thorough knowledge of the theoretical basis of the craft as well as considerable experience in its practice. But to add to this the liking for and understanding of young men, and the skill to interest those who would not have come to classes of their own choice, is no light matter. The good teacher is, of course, born not made; but no branch of an educational system as extensive as the one in Great Britain can hope to staff itself only with born teachers. The large majority in every institution and at every level, from nursery school to university, are those with an appropriate standard of knowledge who have to learn how to teach. In technical institutions, unfortunately, the majority of those teaching at the level of the apprenticeship courses have had little formal training to help them master this difficult art. There are some training colleges for teachers in technical institutions and there are a number of short courses to help those without training to get some idea of methods that they might employ; but, for the most part, technical instructors are appointed without any special training and have to learn by trial and error how to deal with their classes.

The second and third questions are so closely related to one another that they may be considered together, for both are concerned with the level of intellectual ability that can be expected of the pupils in these courses. No matter was more frequently a topic of discussion during interviews with the staffs of technical colleges than the dismay they felt at the low standard of educational achievement they found in the apprentices who registered for the courses. The view was continually expressed that most of the first-year had to be spent in teaching subjects—mathematics and English—that they should have been able to expect would have been mastered before the boys left school. Now as there is no reason to believe that the secondary modern schools are universally incompetent and fail lamentably in their job, it is likely that there are other factors operating which lead to this general disappointment; and there are indeed two very important matters in which such a profound change has taken place that one should not be surprised to find a significant fall in the intellectual standard of boys attending this kind of course.

The first of these profound changes is the result of the Education Act, 1944. Before this Act was passed the opportunities offered to working-class boys to enter a grammar school were severely restricted. Throughout the preceding two or three decades the number of scholarships and free places had of course greatly increased; but nevertheless only a small minority of boys from what were then called Elementary Schools ever managed to get them. It was not only the lack of free vacancies that led to this situation but the economic difficulties of the large number of families who would have liked their boys to have this chance but felt they were not able to afford it. During the twenty years between the two wars the rate of unemployment never fell below 10% of the insured population for more than a very short period, and twice it soared to over 20%. Even those who were in work were constantly faced with the danger that they too might fall into the abyss. With such widespread and chronic unemployment the earnings of those employed were both uncertain and low. Short-time was frequent in many occupations and overtime and bonus earnings were available to only a minority. Even if there had been many more openings in grammar schools it is doubtful whether a much larger number of wage-earning parents would have been willing to take advantage of them. Parents who accepted a free place in a grammar school offered to a boy or girl had to agree to allow the child to remain at school at least until 15 years of age—that is, one year beyond the legal school-leaving age—and many were too eager for their children to begin their contributions to the family exchequer to face this obligation with equanimity.

The situation now is entirely different. The system of 'free places' has disappeared and all fees for secondary education have been abolished. Entry to grammar schools depends on intellectual ability and the boy from the primary school and from the wage-earning family has, legally, as much chance of getting into a grammar school as the candidate from any other school or social group. It might be thought that this remains a statutory right rather than an actual equality of opportunity but according to a recent survey this is not so. Two areas were taken which differed from one another in historical development and occupational distribution— Middlesbrough, Yorkshire, an industrial county borough which has had a chequered economic history, and South West Hertfordshire, a traditionally prosperous district, with an agricultural background amongst which new industries and towns have recently grown up. After an extensive enquiry the conclusions drawn by the authors of this investigation, are: 'If by "ability" we mean "measured intelligence" and by "opportunity" access to grammar schools, then opportunity may be said to be in close relationship with ability in these areas. Though they are not in a strict sense representative areas they are by no means untypical of their kind and we may reasonably conclude that in very many, if not in most, parts of the country the chances of children at a given level of ability entering grammar schools are no longer dependent on their social origin.'[1]

Not only are there more openings available but a larger number of parents are eager and able to take advantage of them. Since the end of the war unemployment has practically disappeared, for the percentage of unemployed has rarely risen above $1\frac{1}{2}\%$ of the insured population; and earnings have increased very much more than would be necessary to compensate for the fall in the value of money. With regular work and good incomes, a large proportion of wage earners are ready to sacrifice any contribution from their adolescent members to the household budget, in order to satisfy their ambition by allowing them to have the education that will open to them new fields of employment. In Middlesbrough 67% of clerical and foremen groups, 53% of skilled workers and 48% of the unskilled, expressed a preference for

[1] J. E. Floud, A. H. Halsey, F. M. Martin, *Social Class and Educational Opportunity*, p. 139.

a grammar school for their boys if they could get it. In South-West Hertfordshire 77% of the clerical workers, 61% of the foremen, 48% of skilled workers and 43% of the unskilled, expressed the same preference. It is not surprising therefore that the proportion of working-class boys in the grammar schools has increased so greatly. The following tables show the change in the social origins of boys attending this type of school.

Father's occupation	Middlesbrough		S.W. Hertfordshire	
	1905–18	1953	1884–1900	1950/3
Professional Workers, Managers, Business Owners	29·8	23·3	23·8	21
Clerical Workers	7·8	7·7	16·6	16
Foremen, Small Shop-keepers, and similar grades	38·6	24·4	48·4	19
Skilled Manual Workers	16·2	30·8	10·8	34
Unskilled Manual Workers	6·6	13·8	0·4	8
Unclassified	1·0	—	—	2
	100	100	100	100

If we take the manual workers alone, whereas at the beginning of this century under 23% of the grammar school places in Middlesbrough were occupied by children of skilled and unskilled manual workers, there were in 1953 44½% from this group ; in S.W. Hertfordshire the proportion had risen from 11% to over 42%.

Here then is one important reason for the comparatively low standard of educational achievement amongst the pupils in craft courses. An enormous number of boys of high intelligence, who would not have had the opportunity to get a grammar school education before the war, now have this chance; but the regulations governing apprenticeship make it almost impossible for any of these boys to be trained for skilled crafts. Theoretically permission can be given for a boy to begin an apprenticeship after the usual age of 16, but it is rare for this to be done. Most employers prefer boys to come to them at 15 so as to serve a probationary period before contracting to train them for five years, and this results in the almost complete exclusion of the more intelligent boys from training as skilled craftsmen. The exclusion is not yet quite complete because there are a number of boys who are un-willing to go to a grammar school, though intelligent enough to get a place; and there are still parents who cannot afford to promise to allow their children to stay on the extra year that is entailed by acceptance of a place in the grammar school, or who have a low opinion of 'all this book learning' and want their children to begin earning as soon as possible. But the majority *do* take the chance when it is offered and are encouraged to do so by their parents; and the trend in this direction is so strong that it is probable that an even more preponderant majority than at present will be drained away from the skilled industries in this way in the future.

A Survey made by the London School of Printing and Graphic Arts in 1950 of the education of their 326 appren-tices (mainly 16–17 years of age) revealed that only 8% had been to a grammar school, and this in a craft which is more likely than most to attract the boy with a literary education; and this is confirmed by the analysis of the educational back-ground of boys registering for National Service in 1955, when on a general average only about 8–9% of those undergoing a training for industry lasting at least three years, were shown to have attended a grammar school. That there are still a certain number who attend grammar schools and yet are able to be apprenticed is due mainly to the fact that, despite the understanding to remain for the full period of the course, a very considerable number of boys leave before its completion. In some cases this is due to a change in the economic circumstances of the family; for example, the father may die and the boy feel obliged to leave in order to help his mother over a difficult period. In other cases the selection has been badly made and the pupil finds himself unable to cope with the standard of work expected of him. Very often when only one boy from a group of friends manages to get a grammar school place he feels lonely and cut off from all his normal associates and is particularly concerned at being cut out of all the leisure-time activities open to his former companions when they begin to earn £2 10s. or £3 a week; pursuits from which a boy with only two or three shillings pocket money, and homework to do, must be excluded. A recent investigation[1] into early school-leaving expressed a great deal of concern over this wastage from the grammar schools and made recommendations which are likely to lead to its decrease. So, here again, the source of supply of the more intelligent boys who still go into craft apprenticeships is likely to dry up still further. In the future, therefore, if apprenticeship regulations remain as they are, if more parents take advantage of the openings offered their children and if a larger proportion of those who go to grammar schools remain to complete the full course, it is certain that an even smaller proportion of 'bright boys' will be entering the craft technical courses than there are at present.

The second profound change which has brought about the present situation is that attendance at technical courses is no longer voluntary. It is part of the agreed schemes of all the industries included in this enquiry that apprentices should be released for the equivalent of a day a week, and the technical colleges are expected to deal with them, whatever their desire to learn and whatever their intellectual capacity. This is one of the very few types of educational provision in which the institution has no power at all to lay down the standard of admission for its pupils. Eager or reluctant, bright or stupid, it has to accept them all. It is perhaps not surprising therefore that so small a proportion reach the standard of achievement set for courses designed for eager pupils attending voluntarily, and presumably ceasing to attend if they find themselves unable to follow instruction.

If apprentices were carefully selected in the first instance this might not prove so great a problem; but as has been seen above, it is in only a tiny minority of cases that any care is taken, and the large majority of boys released for attendance at technical classes have not undergone any form of selective process at all, to determine whether they are capable of profiting from any instruction.

Does this inability to master the theoretical instruction

[1] *Early Leaving*, H.M.S.O. 1954.

mean that they are incompetent workers? Evidently not, and on this matter employers and technical colleges seem to be in agreement. During discussions with people from both groups the same view was continually expressed: 'They are fine lads and good skilled craftsmen. Give them a practical job to do and they do it as well as one could wish.' There are many employers even who do not bother to enquire whether their apprentices have reached the prescribed standard or not, because they can judge from their performance in the workshop whether they are worth their pay, and whether they are likely to be good workers when the term of apprenticeship is over. There seems here to be a very anomalous situation. Is there any sense in prescribing a course of technical instruction for a whole class of workers when evidently both employers and instructors believe it an unnecessary part of the equipment of a skilled and satisfactory workman? Supposing that 95% of medical students failed to pass the qualifying examination of the medical schools, would one still consider them competent doctors and give them a licence to practise? If so, one would have to conclude that there was something wrong, either with medical education or with the standard of the examination, and this conclusion seems the only one that can be reached with regard to the instruction given to craft apprentices and the examinations that they are set. If the boys do indeed make excellent craftsmen despite their poor showing in the technical colleges, then evidently the content of the course is unsuitable and the standard of achievement demanded too high.

Many of the technical colleges are coming to this conclusion, and in some trades proposals have been made for a grading of courses. There are a number of boys capable of reaching Intermediate City and Guilds level and it would be wrong to prevent them from getting the instruction by which they could profit. To lower the standard of all technical instruction for apprentices would be as unjust to the brighter boys as it is now to try to force the general body to understand work beyond their capacity. A two-tier or even three-tier system would get over this problem. Already in a few courses arrangements have been made with the City and

Guilds Institute for the provision of a Craftsman's Certificate (based mainly on a practical examination) which would testify to the holder's competence as a skilled workman in a particular craft. Development along these lines seems to be the most promising course.

VI

THE FUTURE

THE most remarkable fact about the present system of recruiting and training young workers for skilled industry is that in all essential points it is exactly the same as the method introduced more than 800 years ago for an entirely different economy. When this system was formalized by the Statute of Artificers in 1562 it was already old in practice. The earliest extant records of apprenticeship are private contracts between individuals which stipulate for a premium to be paid, or certain years of service to be given in return for specified teaching, and by the thirteenth century this type of contract began to be authorized and regulated by the Guilds. The education provided by the Guilds rested entirely on a domestic basis. Apart from his own sons the master craftsman might have only one apprentice who received board, lodging, clothing, discipline and instruction as one of the family. When he entered a household the apprentice passed under the protection of the Guild, which furnished a Court of Appeal against ill-usage or defective training,[1] and guaranteed ultimate attainment of mastership. When the Statute of Artificers was passed the objective was to make this method of training young workers uniform for all occupations. But this arrangement was not only a technical training, it was the only system of education that existed for the general population. It was the master's responsibility to teach his apprentices much more than his craft; by admitting him to his household he was expected also to initiate him into the customs of society and bring him up in ways of godliness.

[1] *Studies in Economic History*, George Unwin, pp. 95-6.

That modern industry is now entirely different from what it was in the twelfth century, and that it operates in a completely different social environment is a point that it is unnecessary to labour. Yet throughout the 150 years in which modern industry has been developing there has never been a detached investigation into the methods that might prove most suitable for training the younger members of society for the kinds of work that modern industry requires. The old system has been revived without any question being asked of its applicability to a profoundly different situation.

The supervision by the Guilds of the contract between master and apprentice was not exercised solely for the protection of the young worker, nor even to maintain the reputation of the Guild for good workmanship. It was also a method of ensuring that the number of skilled masters in the craft was not excessive. When the trade unions tried to revive the system of apprenticeship in the nineteenth century it was this second function of restricting the numbers engaged in the trade, rather than a consideration of the methods of training young workers, that was their main idea; and this has remained so ever since. Although the factory with hundreds of specialized workers operating complicated machines had taken the place of the master craftsman working with simple hand tools in his own home, and although the apprentice could obviously no longer live as a member of the master's household working with him in the closest co-operation, it was taken for granted that this method of binding a limited number of boys for a period of years would provide them with the instruction and practice they needed to become skilled workers, in exactly the same way as it had done centuries before. Nobody bothered to enquire whether the boys did in fact get any instruction; nobody tested their competence when the period of years they were bound for came to an end; nobody asked if there were any alterations worth considering.

The revival of interest in the training of young workers during the 'forties was equally based on the assumption that the old system of apprenticeship was 'a good thing' and ought to be revived and extended; and all the agreed schemes incorporated the traditional pattern without giving any serious consideration to its suitability to modern needs. Apprenticeship for five years beginning at 16 and ending at 21 has been accepted as if it were a sacred law. Why must every training irrespective of the skills to be learnt take five years? Why must every training end at 21? Such questions, it seems, were never seriously asked. In other kinds of occupation than that of skilled manual work, it is recognized that different periods of time are required to master the essentials sufficiently to take a job as a qualified person. It takes, for example, three years to get a degree in engineering, and six to get one in medicine, and one can learn to be a competent shorthand typist in a year. Yet it was assumed without question that every manual skill needs exactly five years to master.

It is ironic that the very organizations which have used their great political strength to support the wider educational facilities which open professional work to larger social groups, should be the ones that so severely restrict entry to their own fields of employment. There are many young men who, having reached their twenties, wish that they had been trained for more skilled and interesting work than the semi-skilled repetition jobs on which they are engaged. Perhaps they may have had the chance of being trained when they first left school, and rejected it in order to earn a higher immediate wage, or perhaps they did not fully envisage the monotony of the work into which they entered; perhaps there were family difficulties which prevented them from becoming apprentices or they received bad parental advice. As things are, however, having once taken the decision at the early age of 15–16 not to enter apprenticeship, there is, as far as the union regulations are concerned, no going back on it. A man may decide at the age of 30 to study to be a doctor or a lawyer, but unless he makes up his mind before he is 16 to be a fitter, motor mechanic, or carpenter, he has missed his chance for life. The unions' obsession with the age of 21, at which every training must end, makes his entry into the ranks of skilled workers impossible. As has been pointed out earlier, some trades do admit 'dilutees', that is, the upgrading of men from a less skilled range of work in order to overcome severe shortages of manpower; but this is done grudgingly and is hedged round with conditions. Adult apprenticeship as a recognized institution is taboo.

It might be thought that the methods of recruitment and training would not have been revived, nor have managed to exist for so long, had they not proved themselves the most effective way of reaching the desired end. But the experience of other countries shows that the British traditional method of training is not the only way in which qualified workers can be provided for skilled industries. In America, France, Germany and the Netherlands, all countries with a large amount of skilled industry, the methods of training are very different from ours.

In the U.S.A. the problem of training skilled workers is comparatively modern, for throughout the last century the flow of emigrants from European countries was sufficient to supply the needs of industry, and it is only since the restrictions on entry into the States that it has been necessary to consider the training of young people to fill these jobs. There were of course some young men who were born in the States and who entered crafts before the new schemes were inaugurated, but they were a minority and did so generally by picking up their knowledge whilst they were employed. It was not until 1920 that regularized apprenticeship really commenced, and not until 1937 that Congress, recognizing the national interest in the all-round training of skilled workers, adopted the Fitzgerald Act which set up the system which is now in operation. As a result of this late start the American system has not been bound by past tradition, but could be designed and modified to suit the needs of American industry.

To implement this Act a National Bureau of Apprenticeship was established with a representative advisory committee known as the Federal Committee on Apprenticeship appointed by the Secretary of Labour. This government body does not itself organize or carry out training programmes, which are the responsibility of management and workers, but it stimulates voluntary action, gives advice and maintains standards. The Bureau has twelve regional offices and about 200 subordinate offices throughout the States whose job it is to help in the setting up and functioning of Local Joint Apprenticeship Committees representative of individual crafts in the area. There is thus a trained corps of officers available, ready to encourage the States to establish apprenticeship standards which conform to the minimum requirements laid down by the Federal Bureau, to assist in the framing of apprenticeship schemes, and to keep a constant and vigilant eye on the way in which the scheme, once agreed by management and labour, is implemented.

The unions are extremely active in the work of the Local Joint Apprenticeship Committees. These generally meet once a month to deal with recruitment and transfer of apprentices and with any disciplinary action needed in view of the progress reports from schools and employers. Some committees accumulate funds by a levy on employers of 2% on the wages bill for apprentices, in order to enable them to pay the salary of a full-time apprentice supervisor, or to augment the salaries of craft instructors and so on. In some localities the unions also contribute to these funds.

A period of training is not considered to constitute a formal apprenticeship unless it requires at least two years, but the period for full apprenticeship varies from one industry to another—the shortest two years and the longest five; the average is $3\frac{1}{2}$–4 years. The age at which training begins is equally flexible. Naturally enough the majority start when they leave school, which is later than Great Britain. The legal school-leaving age varies from one State to another, but in a large number, and particularly in the industrial States, it is 16, and it is much easier for pupils to stay on beyond this age at vocational, technical, or ordinary high schools until the age of 18 than it is here. As, in addition to the effect of this later age of school attendance, there are a number of States in which the employment of boys and girls under the age of 18 is prohibited in a wide range of industrial occupations, it is easy to see that the age of entry into apprenticeship is likely to be different from that in the United Kingdom. In many States there is no upper age limit for entry at all; in some it is 24 with allowances for higher age limits for ex-servicemen. In a recent survey of apprenticeship the variation in the age of commencing apprenticeship was commonly 18–25 but there were some apprentices who had begun training at considerably later ages than these. In certain circumstances the period of training required for the trade is reduced, for example, in consideration of earlier experience in a related kind of work, or if evidence is available that the trainee has benefited by vocational or technical courses at school; or, indeed, even if, without this, the apprentice shows by his work that he is exceptionally gifted or quick to learn. In every scheme provision has to be made for related class-room instruction of at least four hours a week throughout the whole period of apprenticeship, though it must be pointed out that it is not universal for the apprentice to receive payment for this time, as it is in Britain. Though the main training is gained, as it is here, in the works, supervision is continuous and close. The Local Apprenticeship Committees receive regular progress reports on each individual and in some cases test an apprentice's competence before permitting him to proceed to further training or to pass out as qualified. In some trades (air mechanics, plumbers, etc.) the apprentice must obtain a licence issued by the appropriate public authority before he may take regular employment as a journeyman in the trade. Where this is not obligatory, a certificate is awarded on completion of apprenticeship by the State Apprenticeship Council, or, in some cases, by the Federal Committee on Apprenticeship, and this entitles the holder to be recognized as a skilled worker.

The American system of apprenticeship does not guarantee the same security of employment as the British. If there is a falling off of work, and men have to be discharged, apprentices may be dismissed in an agreed ratio of apprentices to craftsmen. As the apprenticeship schemes did not begin to function until the beginning of World War II and there has been so little unemployment since, no great difficulty has yet arisen on this account, for the Local Joint Committees have easily been able to place apprentices with another employer where a firm has not been able to retain the whole of its labour force. But in a time of general depression this might be more serious.

One way of getting over the insecurity inherent in this agreement has led to an interesting and novel development. Apprentices are sometimes indentured, not to an individual employer, but to the Local Apprenticeship Committee itself, representing a whole industry. This is particularly wide-spread in the building industry and frees the employer from the responsibility for retaining apprentices when the work he has in hand is by its nature intermittent. But it is also of value in overcoming the problem posed by the increasing special-ization of production by firms which concentrate on a narrow range of products and which, with the best will in the world, cannot offer an all-round training to an apprentice. By bind-ing the apprentice to an industry instead of a firm, the Apprenticeship Committee can ensure that the training is adequate because it can move the boy round from one firm to another until he has gained general experience.

In 1951 a Specialist Team consisting of representatives of employers and trade unions in several industries together with representatives of all the nationalized industries, the Ministry of Education and the technical colleges, was sent out from this country to the U.S.A. to report on the training of operatives, and summed up its views on the American apprenticeship system as follows: [1]

'Concerning apprenticeships the Team was probably given more food for thought than about any of the other major aspects of its mission and . . . wishes to commend some of the American practices for consideration in this country.

'The first notable point about the American system is the almost complete disregard of the upper age of prospective apprentices. Men can become apprentices up to even the age of 35 and are not expected to begin before they are 18. This gives great flexibility and avoids the stultifying effect

[1] *Training of Operatives*, 1951, Anglo-American Council on Productivity, pp. 43-4.

of the over-rigid practice in Britain where entry into apprenticeship above the age of 16 is unusual.

'The British system was no doubt evolved in the days when the school-leaving age was lower than it is today to ensure that the period of learning on the job should coincide with the years of adolescent development which are considered to finish at 21. This has much to recommend it if it is assumed that a man should have become a skilled worker at 21 if he is to be one at all. But this assumption seems now to be out of date.

'The Team considers that in many trades the present period of apprenticeship might be shortened if candidates were older on entry. Not only would this imply in most cases that they had spent longer at school but that they had reached years of greater discretion. It is realized that there are difficulties which would deter parents and children from accepting this change, the chief of which is probably the financial necessity for a boy to begin earning money as soon as possible. Employers, too, might be loth to pay apprentices the higher rates to which their age would entitle them. *But the Team feel strongly that the question of age limits and periods of training for apprentices should be re-examined very carefully by all industries, particularly now that compulsory National Service has become a permanent feature of British life.*

'The American practice of awarding credits to apprentices for work at vocational schools has been noted before in this Report. These credits enable an apprentice to shorten the period of his shop training by a considerable extent and the system appeared to the Team to have much to recommend it, although it seemed also to be open to abuses. *The Team recommends that the question of giving credits to apprentices in this way should also be investigated by those industries that have not already done so, especially if it can be considered in conjunction with the Recommendation contained in the previous paragraph.*

'One of the methods for organizing effective apprentice training in the U.S., which has already been described in Section 5,[1] impressed the members of the Team very

[1] The reference is to Section 5 of the Report 'Training of Operatives'.

favourably. This is the way in which local joint apprenticeship committees are used. Similar committees exist in this
country, but in general their effectiveness is slight compared with that of their American counterparts, chiefly
because they seldom exercise real authority over either
employer or apprentice. The frequent practice in America,
particularly in the building industry, of indenturing an
apprentice, not to an employer but to the local joint
apprenticeship committee, gives the committee just the
power of control which it would otherwise lack. Another
advantage of this system is that it makes it possible to
ensure that an apprentice receives a properly balanced
training, even though the plants in which he works are
small. This plan appears to open up considerable possibilities in Britain, where the problem of apprenticeship in
small firms is a very pressing one. *The idea of promoting the
system whereby the indenture is made between the apprentice and
the local committee has received attention by certain industries in
this country, but it is recommended that it should be given careful
consideration by others.*

'Organized labour in America plays a much greater part
in apprentice training than it does in the U.K. The Team
felt in one or two of the plants visited that the management
were possibly leaving too much of the responsibility to the
union representatives. Nevertheless, the attitude of the
unions towards apprentice training is good. They are
jealous of the standing of a skilled ticket, the award of
which is of real significance to a worker. *Some unions in this
country might, with advantage to employer and employed, insist
upon higher standards for admission to the ranks of their skilled
workers.*'

In France the method of dealing with this same problem
is entirely different from that of both England and America.
In the early part of this century the training of skilled workers
was in a very unsatisfactory state. Guild regulations had retained their force in France much longer than in the United
Kingdom and the efforts to replace their supervision during

the nineteenth century by educational or by union control did not prove successful. Until comparatively recently most French industry was fairly small-scale and it was not difficult for apprenticeship regulations to be evaded. After the first World War an effort was made to provide systematic training through trade schools, the funds for which were raised by a *taxe d'apprentissage* levied on the wages bill; but it was not until the recent war that a nationwide system was established on the foundations that had been earlier laid. The great impetus came with the need for the rapid rebuilding of a shattered economy after the Liberation. Few skilled workers had been trained during the war itself and when hostilities ended many employers were afraid to commit themselves to a long period of training for young people, when they had so little idea what the future held for them. The Technical Section of the Ministry of Education therefore took over the job of providing a complete craft training in a full-time course lasting three years and covering a wide range of skills.

Their *centres d'apprentissage*, which are a cross between a school and a factory, are now found all over France and cater for about 200,000 young people. They are governed by local committees consisting of one-third each of representatives of local employers, trade unions and the Ministry of Education. In addition to these state institutions there are several hundred similar centres run entirely by industry. Pupils begin their training when they leave school at 14 plus and for the first six months are taught the elements of a number of related trades, after which they begin to specialize. The course leads to an examination at the end of three years and those who pass. gain a *certificat d'aptitude professionnelle* which entitles them to receive the rate of pay of a qualified skilled worker.[1]

Technical education in Germany has a long history but it has been considerably reorganized in the post-war period. In Western Germany 75% of children leave school at 14 and go to work, but for the next three years, or until the end of

[1] See *Technical Education for Adolescents*, C. H. Dobinson, and B.A.C.I.E., *Technical Education in France*, June, 1954, for further details of this Scheme.

apprenticeship, whichever time is the later, it is compulsory
to attend a vocational school for one day a week. The proportion of apprentices is higher than in England, for many
trades are classified as skilled occupations which here are not
placed in that category. Apprenticeship lasts for 3–3½ years
and concludes with an examination held by the Local
Chamber of Industry and Trade. Tests at regular intervals
are a feature of all apprenticeship, given sometimes once a
month, sometimes at three-monthly intervals. If the apprentice fails in either the practical or theoretical final examination he is allowed another try, but if he fails again he is
relegated to the ranks of unskilled labour. If he succeeds, he
is given the Skilled Workers' Certificate which entitles him
to higher rates of pay. Collective Training Centres have been
established to meet the problem of the small or medium-sized
firm. These are set up by the local authorities with strong
trade union support and are subsidized by the West German
Government. Firms send apprentices to them on the understanding that towards the end of the course the needs of the
firm will receive special consideration in their training.

Apprentices are not paid a wage but are given financial
assistance by the employer whilst learning their skill. If the
amount is inadequate (because of family poverty, for example) the Government may make a grant. It was recently
announced, for instance, that the Senate of West Berlin
contributed 2,000,000DM. (£250,000) to a special fund
which enables small firms to accept apprentices. Since the
establishment of this fund 13,500 more places have been
created for apprentices in West Berlin, bringing the total to
52,000.[1]

In the Netherlands a boy who contemplates entering a
skilled industry spends the last two years of his compulsory
eight years' schooling at a junior technical school at which he
receives his basic skills. He then enters full-time employment

[1] For further details, see B.A.C.I.E. Journal, September/October, 1953,
Technical Education in Western Germany, J. Newton; B.A.C.I.E. Journal, June,
1954, *Industrial Training and Education in Western Germany*, E. N. Marriott;
Times Educational Supplement, January 17, 1955.

and serves an apprenticeship for two or three years. If he has not been through the junior technical school, but enters industry straight from the elementary school the apprenticeship is prolonged by one year (or in some cases two years). Day Release for full-time instruction is not universal, but is extending.

Both the technical education provided for the apprentice, and his final certification as a skilled craftsman, are mainly governed by the requirements of one of the 28 Joint (employer and trade union) Trade Federations. BEMETEL (Federation for Technical Education in the Metal and Electro-Technical Industries) is one of the best-known of these federations and its scheme may be taken as typical. BEMETEL has about 900 member firms where metal workers are trained. These include not only works belonging to the metal and electro-technical industries themselves, but also other establishments which need metal workers for their maintenance and repair shops, for example, Royal Dutch Air Lines, Netherlands Railways, public utilities, textile and paper mills. BEMETEL supervises the training and examination of some 8,000 apprentices working within 75 different trades. There is no age limit for becoming an apprentice and at present about 1,200 of these 8,000 are adults over the age of 21, but BEMETEL sets the minimum requirements for the various trades. Each apprentice, no matter the age at which he begins or the type of factory in which he works, knows he must attain the level of craftsmanship required by the final examination if he is to continue to be employed. BEMETEL employs a body of 26 full-time instructors whose chief task is to give advice about new training methods to any interested firm or person. The final examinations are held twice a year and for each examination the candidates have to do the same test-pieces in their own workshops under supervision. In addition they are set a number of questions bearing on their work, which must be answered in writing. The examinations are conducted by a board of experts selected from industry itself and from the technical schools, but appointed by the Ministry of Education on advice from BEMETEL. Not until this final examination has been successfully passed does a boy rank as a skilled worker entitled to receive the rates of pay appropriate to his trade.[1]

It is not suggested that all these schemes are superior to the methods of training used in this country. They are sketched as evidence that other methods are possible and that there may be something to be learnt from the ways in which other industrial countries deal with problems similar to those with which we are faced. The present investigator has no means of knowing how far these methods are successful in achieving all they set out to do. But what is certain is that all the countries named have very big industrial enterprises which depend on skilled work, and that presumably therefore these methods of recruiting and training their skilled personnel cannot be entirely unsuccessful. Yet in none of them is the period of training as long as in this country and in none is there the rigid insistence on an age limit—upper or lower; and in the three European countries named the worker is allowed to claim the status and pay of a skilled man only after passing a test which shows his competence. There is at least food for thought in these facts.

The position in this country is serious and is likely to become more so. On the one hand there is a persistent shortage of skilled workers; on the other a dearth of facilities for training a new supply. In all the industries included in this survey the lack of training places has become evident, and it seems fairly clear that present methods of training involve the small and medium-sized firms in a burden they are unwilling to shoulder. (Lack of apprenticeship vacancies in the large firms in the building industry is due primarily to the mobile character of the work, which accounts for this industry showing somewhat unusual features.) No estimates are available of the 'net costs' of employing apprentices, and the difficulty the investigator experienced in getting any information on this point leads to the belief that few firms have attempted to calculate in any adequate way the relationship between the apprentice's output during the five years of training and the expense incurred by the employer. The figure given by Mr.

[1] B.A.C.I.E. Journal, July/August, 1953, *Apprenticeship Training in the Netherlands*, G. C. M. Hardebeck.

Harvey Frost (see Chapter IV) was an estimate based on the experience of his own firm and he pointed out that there would be wide variations from one firm to another.[1] But the fact that so large a number of firms are unwilling to undertake the work shows that, however rough and ready the estimates made, there is a widespread belief that the employment of apprentices involves a loss. In the large firms the loss is recognized though not precisely assessed; but it is so small a proportion of general costs of production as to be borne with comparative equanimity in order to ensure a supply of skilled workers for the future. Yet even amongst the large firms there is a strong belief that it is only during the last year or two that the apprentice makes a net contribution to production, so that these in a sense compensate for the losses incurred during the first three years. It was this belief that led so many during discussions to support the long period of apprenticeship, rather than any conviction that a boy could not learn the skills in a shorter time.

It is only in the post-war period that the burden of training has become so heavy. In the past, boy labour was so cheap that there is no doubt that it was shamefully exploited in very many firms. Faced with the difficulty of raising the adolescent rates of pay the unions were certainly right to use all their efforts to restrict the number of youths a firm could have on its strength, either by maintaining a ratio of apprentices to craftsmen or by making apprenticeship less attractive through the long period of training. But now the position is profoundly different. The shortage of young people (due to the low birth-rate of the 'thirties) in a world of full employment has pushed up earnings of adolescents more than those of adults. Between 1947 and 1956 the wage rates of young people had risen 78% compared with a rise of 63% for men and earnings by an even larger amount.[2] No firm could hope to get any apprentices unless the pay offered was at least

[1] The Bureau of Apprenticeship of the United States Department of Labor publishes a pamphlet *Evaluating Apprentices*, which gives elaborate and detailed advice to firms on how to determine the cost of apprenticeship and to record the skill they acquire during training. But there is nothing of the sort available in Britain.

[2] Annual Abstract of Statistics, 1956.

comparable with the earnings of boys in semi-skilled employment, though the latter are employed for their output and the apprentice is receiving instruction. The firm employing the apprentices must needs look on it as a form of capital investment which will bring returns only in the future; otherwise he will not get any young workers to sign on at all. When to the high rates of pay for boys producing little, if anything, to contribute to the firm's output, are added the loss of one complete day's work per week, and the constant interruption of the work schedules in the workshop by the absence of the boy at technical classes, it is no wonder that so large a number of establishments find apprentices more trouble and expense than they are willing to incur.

It is unlikely that the situation will change in this respect and unless it does it is improbable that any kind of exhortation or nagging will induce employers to offer a much larger number of vacancies for apprentices. Under the present system therefore the deficiency in training vacancies is likely to be permanent.

In the meantime, however, the number of young people about to enter employment is increasing. 1956 saw the number of boys attaining the age of 15 at its lowest level, for this still represented the low birth-rate of the earlier period. But from that year there will be a sharp rise as a result of the 'bulge' in the birth-rate which took place between 1942 and 1947. The number of boys in Great Britain estimated to reach the age of 15 is given in the following table:[1]

Year	Thousands	Year	Thousands
1954	328	1962	475
1955	318	1963	419
1956	312	1964	398
1957	346	1965	382
1958	364	1966	373
1959	396	1967	372
1960	359	1968	380
1961	438		

It can be seen therefore that in the next ten years the number entering employment will be considerably higher

[1] C.Y.E.E Memorandum 23, July, 1956.

than those of the comparable age group in recent years. Not all of the young people in this table will be available for employment. But unless the legal school-leaving age is raised it is probable that the proportions of those staying for further education will not be appreciably different from what they have been in the recent past. As things are at present therefore there will be many more anxious to be trained for skilled work, but unless there are fundamental changes in the apprenticeship system there will not be a corresponding increase in the vacancies available for training this much larger number of boys.

What fundamental changes might be introduced? An investigator who has no practical experience of industry cannot make positive suggestions; but there are a number of ideas that have emerged from the results of the survey which may be put forward for consideration. The first and most obvious suggestion is that the period of training should be shortened. In no other country is so long a period demanded, and presumably therefore it is not essential for the training of a skilled worker. Nor can it reasonably be maintained that it requires just five years to master a skill irrespective of the craft to be learned. Such a remarkable coincidence seems at least unlikely, and indeed during discussions this point was rarely raised. The unions insist on five years first and foremost because it is traditional, and largely because of the extraordinary, almost obsessional, relationship in the minds of industrial negotiators between the age of 21 and the receipt of adult occupational rates of pay. But there is also the belief that this prolonged period of training acts as a brake on entry so that even where, as in the majority of skilled trades today, the ratio of apprentices to craftsmen is not observed, a shorter period of training might lead, it is thought, to too large or too rapid an increase in the supply of qualified workers. On the other hand, the employers agree because, as has been shown, they hope to compensate for the losses on training during the first three years by the output of the last two. If apprenticeship were reduced to, say, three years, there would be no chance of thus offsetting their losses.

Such a reduction in the length of training would have a

number of advantages. Even if there were no flexibility introduced into the upper age limits, and it was still obligatory for all apprenticeship to be completed by the age of 21, it would allow entry up to the age of 18. Not only would this mean that the great decision which affects a man's employment career for the next fifty years would not have to be made at so early an age as at present, but it would also allow those who have remained longer in full-time education to offer themselves as apprentices instead of, as now, being completely excluded. It is fairly certain that neither employers nor unions have yet faced the revolutionary effects of the 1944 Education Act. As it took a few years for the new selection processes to get into their strides, the movement of the more intellectually able boys into grammar schools has only recently reached the stage when it begins to be fully effective. The number of boys who have commenced an apprenticeship during the last five or six years whilst this has being going on, form an insignificant proportion of the total skilled labour force, and industry does not yet realize that the high quality of so many of its adult workers is the result of the lack of educational opportunity available when they were young. When they compare their new apprentices with those of earlier periods they are inclined to censure the younger generation ('Things are not what they were when I was a boy'), or more often to throw the blame on the schools for not providing them with abler and better educated boys as trainees for the future. What they have so far not realized is that they have effectively excluded the abler boys by their own action, and that consequently as the new entrants who, of necessity, are now drawn from the less intellectually able section of school-leavers gradually become a larger and larger proportion of the total of skilled craftsmen, it is absolutely certain that there will be a decline in the general average of ability in the skilled labour force.

Does this matter? it may be asked. If these boys make competent craftsmen would it not be wasteful to draw into their ranks boys of greater ability? Or even if the regulations allowed it, would any large number of boys clever enough to gain admission to the grammar schools wish to become apprentices? Nobody, and certainly no outsider, can give an authoritative answer to either of these questions. But there are certain matters related to such questions that are worth remembering. The first is that there are certainly many boys with the intellectual ability to get places in a grammar school who have neither the capacity nor the wish to continue their education beyond, say, 17, and whose interest is founded much more firmly in practical skills than in clerical or in professional work. Engineering, in all its many branches, printing and lithography, etc. excite the imagination of a very large number of boys who are unwilling to aspire to higher technological qualifications, but who would certainly be attracted to skilled work if it could promise a chance of promotion for the future.

This possibility of promotion to work of greater responsibility underlies the second point to be considered. One of the most important developments of recent years is the extent to which promotion from the shop floor to the managerial ranks has become possible. This has been illustrated in a recent Survey made by the Acton Trust into the background of managers in 27 of the largest firms in the country (i.e. those employing over 10,000 people) which revealed that 21% of all those in managerial posts had started out as manual employees (including craft apprentices). It would be a disastrous and retrograde step if this tendency were reversed. But if the entry into skilled crafts is confined to those of lower intellectual ability such a reversal is almost bound to take place, and we should bring into being a rigidity of social stratification in industry even greater than the one from which we are now so slowly and so painfully emerging.

If the period of apprenticeship were considerably reduced, other changes would have to follow. One of the most startling facts that emerges from this enquiry is that apprentices are rarely, if ever, actually *taught* their trade. Even in the firms with well-organized Works Schools in which preliminary instruction is given, and with complex progressive work schedules supervised by full-time Directors of Training or Apprentice Masters, where the whole administrative set-up is admirable, the actual teaching of apprentices seems to be non-existent. No boy can become a skilled worker solely by teaching, without practising the job himself, but he is likely to become more skilled, more quickly, if he is shown what to do and how to do it, with some explanation of the snags to be avoided. 'There never was a more false belief,' said an eminent American at a Chicago conference on this topic 'than to think than if you get a boy in a shop with a foreman he is going to get the finest kind of training. The foreman is not always a good teacher. If the youth gets a good foreman he gets good training. If he gets a bad foreman he gets bad training.'[1] This is the same opinion, differently expressed, as that of the master printer quoted earlier. There is no doubt therefore that if training is to be more concentrated, more and better instruction is necessary.

How can such improved instruction be obtained? To suggest, as did most of the Memoranda inaugurating the new schemes, that boys should always be put in the charge of craftsmen with a liking for teaching and the ability to explain things clearly to their pupils, is simply to refuse to recognize the difficulty inherent in the situation. Even in the big firms there are few such men available, and in the small firms, even if there happened to be a skilled man with a flair for teaching, he cannot afford to take time off to explain as fully as is required just what he is doing. Another method must be found to make certain that apprentices are taught the rudiments of their skills, instead of being left to pick them up.

A possible way out of the difficulty might be to establish for craft apprentices a 'sandwich system' similar to that which is becoming increasingly popular for the training of technical apprentices. The details of the system vary from firm to firm and from industry to industry but the principles are the same —to alternate periods of full-time instruction in a Technical College with full-time supervised practical work in employment. In most cases the scheme is selective: the youths chosen are those who have already passed the G.C.E. in appropriate science subjects and have given evidence of ability to reach a good standard during the first year of their training. This is understandable, for the firms continue to pay full wages

[1] *Training of Operatives*, 1951. Anglo-American Council on Productivity, p. 25.

during the periods when the apprentice is at College, which may be six or nine months at a time: and naturally enough they want some guarantee that this investment in the training of their future technicians is likely to be worth its cost.

Some similar but less ambitious scheme might be practicable for craft apprentices. Instead of being released for one day a week to attend classes they might be required to attend the college for three or four weeks at a time. At present they attend only during college terms, which means that they receive about 40 days' instruction in the year—which equals about eight weeks full time. If this instruction was 'sandwiched' between periods of employment, one month of instruction followed by five months of employment in the works of the firm to which they are indentured, would provide the same number of days as they have now, but would almost certainly be of very much greater benefit to them. The alternation of 'works' and 'technical college' would enable the apprentice to get specific teaching in the skills he needs to acquire together with some understanding of the scientific principles on which they are based; and in such circumstances the lack of any teaching during the workshop periods would be of less consequence. The employing firm would thus be relieved of the irksome task of trying to find a skilled workman willing to look after a pupil.

It is possible that employers might jib at paying wages for a month in which they were getting nothing concrete in return, even though the annual amount of paid 'learning time' was no greater than it is now. In this case, if apprenticeship came to be looked upon primarily as *training* rather than as *employment* the instruction periods might be allowed to attract payment out of collective funds, whether these were provided by the State as part of its educational programme, or by the industry itself through a levy on employers as a group.

A reduction in the period of training would have one very great additional advantage in that it would make more possible the removal of the upper age limit and open the door to skilled work to adults over the age of 21. Such 'Adult Apprenticeship' is in fact virtually allowed now in those industries, such as engineering, which permit upgrading from the ranks of the semi-skilled in the effort to overcome the acute manpower shortage. But by agreement the names of such dilutees must be kept on a special register so that they can be the first to be dismissed if it becomes necessary to reduce the number employed. The admission that such upgrading is possible is confirmation of the fact that skill can be acquired in a shorter period than is now required by the regulations, and is evidence that the refusal to allow apprenticeship to be entered at a later age is a method of restricting numbers rather than of maintaining standards of workmanship. Is there any other reason for retaining this group as a permanently inferior class except that of retaining some advantage for those who have entered skilled work by the traditional avenues? And yet the maintenance of a dilutees' register has this effect of relegating one group of skilled men permanently to a lower status.

In other industrial European countries, as has been shown, the apprentice is not considered fully qualified until he has passed a test of his competence—a test imposed by a specially constituted examining body representing both industry and educational institutions. In this country there is no test at all. The mere passage of time is the only qualification. The boy may be a poor workman, badly taught and employed exclusively on a narrow range of activities instead of moving over the whole range of skills; but when he reaches the age of 21 he is automatically qualified as a skilled craftsman and is admitted to the appropriate trade union. If some test of competence were imposed at the end of apprenticeship the difficulty of the adult apprentice might more easily be overcome. Instead of specifying the period to be spent in training, the standard of workmanship of which he showed himself capable might be the test. A man who is working even on less skilled jobs acquires a great deal of knowledge that the apprentice must learn during his period of training—the nature of the material, the layout of the works, the handling of tools with precision and so on. If such a man is quick in the uptake and has ambition, he can by attendance at evening classes raise himself to the level of the skilled worker. If he can pass the examination, is there any good reason why he should not be admitted to the ranks of the skilled craftsman?

The shortening of the period of apprenticeship would not remove the difficulty under which the small and medium-sized firm now labours in providing training facilities. Indeed it might increase them, for there would be less time in which the apprentices' output could compensate for earlier losses and a more concentrated training would require more direct teaching and supervision. The only way out of this difficulty is for responsibility for the apprentice to be taken off the individual firm. How could this be achieved? It might be done if craft training became a function of the educational system instead of industry. In the eighteenth century, for example, many doctors were trained for their profession by being apprenticed to a general practitioner, but they are now educated at medical schools and get their practice in hospitals not as paid employees but as one part of their educational period. Such a transfer of functions might be possible in training skilled workers, and that it is so is shown by what is done in France; but it has some grave disadvantages. Industrial techniques change very rapidly and it is important that workers should be trained in new methods rather than old. It is true that not every employer is in the vanguard in introducing new methods, but unless he is prepared to adapt his works to some extent he is likely to be left behind in the competition for markets. Training workshops run by education authorities might be more progressive than the average run of employers if they are run by enlightened bodies with plenty of money at their command; but there might, on the contrary, be a temptation to postpone the introduction of new machines and similar equipment because of the difficulty of justifying the heavy cost to taxpayers. Equally important perhaps is the difference in the psychological climate of an industrial enterprise and of an educational institution. A business firm makes goods which it hopes to sell at a profit and it must keep one eye on the market and the other on its costs. If it is to continue to be solvent it must produce in such a way that market prices cover costs of production, and that means that the quality of workmanship demanded must be constantly and directly related to the price the final product fetches in the market. An educational institution, on the other hand, is usually more concerned with the quality of the work done than with its cost of production in relation to its marketable value. 'If a thing is worth doing it is worth doing well' is a general educational maxim but in the economic world it is not always sound. It is not worth while to put into a job a higher standard of workmanship than is required for the purpose it is intended to serve; it is, for example, wasteful to put costly materials and workmanship into something that is intended to have a very short life, for example, a Christmas cracker. For this reason training for skilled work in the realistic conditions of a productive establishment has its advantages. The sandwich system already discussed would get over this difficulty.

Another way in which the responsibility for training might be taken off the individual firm is by instituting a system of group apprenticeship such as is now being tried by Industrial Administration (R. & A.) Ltd. (see Chapter IV). Such a system has undoubted advantages, but as it depends on initiative being taken by a large number of groups of firms prepared to act together it is likely to be rather slow in development.

A scheme based on the same idea but which has greater potentialities is 'Apprenticeship to an Industry' instead of apprenticeship to a firm—such as has been introduced in the building industry in the U.S.A. Such a method has a great deal to commend it and seems the most constructive way out of present difficulties. It has the great value that not only does it remove the strain and expense of training from the individual firm but it allows of better all-round experience for the apprentice. The degree of specialization reached by many small firms is so great that, with the best will in the world towards their apprentices, they cannot provide a wide range of activities for them. As things are now, the exchange of apprentices between firms *can* take place but it involves so much bother and organization that few small firms can spare the time and personnel to deal with it. If a boy were apprenticed to an industry it would be much easier for arrangements to be made for him to move from firm to firm until he had acquired all-round knowledge. For such a scheme to be successful certain conditions would be essential:

(1) The responsible body must be jointly representative of the industry, both employers and unions. In America the Local Joint Apprenticeship Committee acts in this way. In this country a similar organization is already available in most industries but the committees would need to be very much more active bodies than they are at present if they were to perform such a function adequately.

(2) The responsible body, say the Local Joint Apprenticeship Committee, would sign the indentures instead of any individual employer and would thus become responsible for paying the wages of the apprentice and supervising his training.

(3) The Joint Apprenticeship Committee would require a full-time corps of officials to act as instructors and supervisors and to decide where to place and when to move him.

(4) The firm with which the boy was placed would pay an appropriate sum into the funds of the Joint Apprenticeship Committee in lieu of the wages for which it would be responsible under the present system.

The scheme outlined above is similar to that devised by BEMETEL, whose plan seems particularly worthy of examination as a possible development for the small firm in this country.

The difficulties encountered by the specialist firm in providing all-round training lead to a further question: 'Is this all-round training still required by all skilled craftsmen?' One of the problems faced by the building industry in recent years, for example, has been the shortage of skill of very high quality because during so long a period there was no outlet for such skills. As all the building allowed during the war and immediate post-war years was of an essentially utilitarian character there was no opportunity for men to acquire or practise the highly skilled techniques needed in buildings which are constructed to individual requirements of a more luxurious type. But even now that restrictions on building have been removed, the greater part of the constructional work done by the industry remains of the functional variety in which there is a large element of standardization of units in order to cut costs. In such circumstances a very considerable proportion of building craftsmen are needed, whose higher skills if they had acquired them, would rarely, if ever, be called upon. In engineering again there is a great deal of production which demands some skill, but neither the variety nor the level of skill of the highest order. Is there not some point in recognizing this fundamental change in the pattern of industrial production and of adjusting to it by training a hierarchy of skills of varying levels instead of demanding that all, irrespective of the work they will do for the rest of their lives, should be trained to the same degree? Universities recognize these differences in levels of education by offering pass degrees and general degrees as well as honours, and in such a profession as teaching there are opportunities for employment for persons holding all these different types of qualification. Might not a similar grading in craft skills be possible and economic?

If, as was suggested earlier, admission to the ranks of skilled workers were made as the result of a test of competence instead of by the passage of time, such a hierarchy of skills need not impose any handicap on the progress of an ambitious worker. A man who had reached only a low level of skill might, if he wished, by attendance at evening classes or otherwise, gain the extra experience that would enable him to pass a test for a higher range; whilst those who felt satisfied with the level they had reached would not have to endure the constant sense of frustration of the man who has spent valuable years in acquiring skills that he is never called upon to exercise in his employment.

That some such grading of skills seems called for is evidenced both by the large number of firms employing the men accepted as skilled workers but whose type of production is narrowly specialized, and by the problem facing the technical colleges in providing courses suitable at one and the same time both for those who reach the prescribed standard and for the overwhelming majority who do not. If we were willing to recognize the fact that a very large number of boys have not the capacity to master the knowledge required by the highest grade of skill, it would be possible to provide for them an education that was more valuable because more suited to their aptitudes. When the new apprenticeship schemes were agreed it was believed that the County Colleges were about to be established, and that all young people, and not only apprentices, would be released from paid work for a day a week in order to continue their education. If this had happened it is possible that the technical instruction of apprentices would be very different in design from what it is now, because it would have been recognized as part of the general educational provision for young people. As it is, courses that were designed for an entirely different purpose have been flooded by pupils for whom they were not planned, with the results noted in Chapter V, of constant failure. One shudders to think what the effect is on an unfortunate boy forced to repeat year after year the same course which he is not capable of understanding. How he must long for his eighteenth birthday! And, similarly, one's sympathy goes out to the even more unfortunate instructor, faced year after year by a class of boys completely incapable of grasping the theories he tries to teach them, and that he must continue to teach for the sake of the clever few amongst them. He knows them to be eager and useful workers; it is not their fault that they cannot reach the level of understanding the courses demand. How much more sensible it would seem to be to accept this fact of differences in human ability and cater for them in industrial training as we now do in formal education. If the time and effort now spent in the fruitless attempt to teach boys scientific principles beyond their comprehension were used in more general education, it is likely that the process would be very much more enjoyable both to pupils and teachers, and the results much more valuable to society.

APPENDIX

QUESTIONNAIRE SENT TO ENGINEERING FIRMS

BEDFORD COLLEGE, UNIVERSITY OF LONDON
REGENTS PARK, N.W.1

Dear Sirs,

I write to ask if you will be good enough to help in an enquiry I am making. Since the war apprenticeship schemes have been introduced into some industries and in others, existing schemes have been further developed, with the aim of ensuring an adequate supply of skilled workers. I am now trying to collect information which will allow an assessment of the present position to be made.

My enquiry is confined to the industries which employ the largest proportion of skilled workers—engineering,[1] shipbuilding, printing, building and motor repair: and this questionnaire is being sent to firms of different sizes in each of these industries.

With the exception of the questions specifying different crafts, the questionnaire is the same for all industries and you may find, therefore, that some of the questions do not relate directly to the particular conditions of your industry. I should be most grateful, however, if you would fill in as much of the questionnaire as possible, whether you employ apprentices or not, and return it to me in the enclosed stamped envelope.

I should like to assure you that any information you give will be regarded as strictly confidential and that no name, nor any detail connected with a firm, will be published without written permission of the firm concerned.

Yours faithfully,

GERTRUDE WILLIAMS

---

[1] The questionnaire printed is that for engineering firms. There are slight variations between the different trades.

A

1. TOTAL NUMBER EMPLOYED BY THE FIRM

(a) Administrative, Technical and Clerical Employees which includes directors (other than those paid by fee only), managers, superintendents, works foremen; research, experimental, development, technical and design employees (other than operatives), draughtsmen, tracers, travellers, and office (including works office) employees

(b) Operatives
which includes all other classes of employees, that is, broadly speaking, all manual workers. These figures should include all those employed in or about the factory or works; inspectors, viewers, etc., operatives employed in transport work, stores and warehouses; operatives engaged on outside work of erection, fitting, etc., cleaners

2. AGE CLASSIFICATION

(a) The number of Administrative, Technical, and Clerical employees (as defined above) under 21 years of age

(b) The number of Operatives (as defined above) under 21 years of age

3. THE NUMBER OF CRAFT APPRENTICES

employed by the firm at the time of receiving this questionnaire

---

In answering many of the questions that follow please tick the answer which applies in your case

4. AGE RESTRICTION

Do you accept as craft apprentices boys of 16 years of age and over?   YES.... NO....

5. WAITING LIST

(a) Have you a waiting list of boys desiring to be apprentices on your firm?   YES.... NO....

(b) If so, how many boys are there on this waiting list? ....

(c) Does this indicate a long standing surplus of applicants for craft apprenticeships?   YES.... NO....

(d) In relation to which skilled crafts does this surplus demand for apprenticeships apply?..................

6. UNFILLED VACANCIES

(a) How many unfilled craft apprenticeship vacancies are there on your firm at the time of receiving this questionnaire? ....

(b) Does this indicate a long-standing shortage of applicants for craft apprenticeships?   YES.... NO....

(c) If so, in relation to which skilled crafts does this shortage mainly apply?

....

7. SHORTAGE OF ADULT CRAFTSMEN

(a) Is your firm finding a shortage of ADULT skilled Craftsmen?   YES.... NO....

(b) If so, in relation to which skilled crafts does this shortage mainly apply?

....

8. CRAFT APPRENTICE INSTRUCTION

(a) How many of your craft apprentices attend BOTH Part-Time Day Release and Evening Classes?   ....

How many of these attend as a compulsory condition of their apprenticeship engagement?   ....

(b) How many of your craft apprentices attend ONLY Part-Time Day Release classes?   ....

How many of these attend as a compulsory condition of their apprenticeship engagement?   ....

(c) How many of your craft apprentices attend ONLY Evening Technical classes?   ....

How many of these attend as a compulsory condition of their apprenticeship engagement?   ....

9. APPRENTICE CRAFT COURSES

How many of your craft apprentices attending Part-Time Day Release classes are receiving:

(a) Craft courses........(b) City and Guilds courses........
(c) National Certificate courses........

10. APPRENTICESHIP CERTIFICATE

Are your craft apprentices awarded a Certificate of Completion on the satisfactory completion of their apprenticeship period?   YES.... NO....

11. FIRMS REPRESENTATION

(a) Is your firm represented on the governing body of the local Technical College or Institute?   YES.... NO....

(b) Is your firm consulted on matters dealing with the content of technical courses for craft apprentices at the local Technical College or Institute?   YES.... NO....

(c) Is the local Employers Association to which you belong represented on the governing body of the local Technical College or Institute?   YES.... NO....

12. JOINT APPRENTICESHIP COMMITTEE

Is your firm represented on a local Joint Apprenticeship Committee for recruitment and training?   YES.... NO....

13. YOUTH EMPLOYMENT SERVICE

Does your firm inform the local Youth Employment Service of ALL, SOME, or NONE of its craft apprenticeship vacancies?   ALL.... SOME.... NONE....

14. RECRUITMENT

Does your firm use any of the following methods of recruitment:

Advertisement in the local press or trade papers   YES.... NO....
Advertisement within the firm   YES.... NO....
Propaganda to schools   YES.... NO....

B *Please fill in the following details for 1955 and then as many of other years as possible*

	1955	1954	1953	1952	1951
1. The total number of craft apprentices on the firm as at Jan. 1 in each of the following years					
2. The number of craft apprentices under indenture or other form of written agreement as at Jan. 1 in each of the following years					
3. The number of craft apprentices registered on a Regional or National register as at Jan. 1 in each of the following years					
4. The number of your craft apprentices attending BOTH Day Release and Evening Classes as at Jan. 1 in each of the following years					
5. The number of your craft apprentices attending ONLY Part-Time Day Release classes as at Jan. 1 in each of the following years					
6. The number of your craft apprentices attending ONLY Evening Classes as at Jan. 1 in each of the following years					
7. The number of your craft apprentices *over* 18 years of age attending Day Release Classes as at Jan. 1 in each of the following years					
8. The number of your craft apprentices holding or preparing for City and Guilds certificates as at Jan. 1 in each of the following years					
9. The number of your craft apprentices holding or preparing for National Certificates as at Jan. 1 in each of the following years					
10. The number of your craft apprentices who on reaching the age of 18 years were deferred from National Service in each of the following years					
11. The number of your craft apprentices who on reaching the age of 18 years were NOT deferred from National Service in each of the following years					
12 The number of craft apprentices whose apprenticeship with your firm was *cancelled* before the end of their apprenticeship period for reasons *other* than transfer to other firms, in each of the following years					

C *Please fill in as many of the following details as may apply to your firm*

If you recruit apprentices to crafts in addition to those shown in Column 1, please add these crafts to the bottom of Column 1 and fill in the relevant details

1 ENGINEERING CRAFTS	2 No. of adult skilled craftsmen employed on 1 Jan. 1955 in each craft in Col. 1	3 No. of adult skilled craftsmen employed on 1 Jan. 1955 in each craft in Col. 1 who served a recognized apprenticeship with your firm	4 No. of adult skilled craftsmen employed on 1 Jan. 1955 in each trade in Col. 1 who served a recognized apprenticeship with other firms	5 No. of craft apprentices employed on 1 Jan. 1955 in each craft in Col. 1	6 No. of these craft apprentices employed under indenture or other form of written agreement on 1 Jan. 1955 in each craft in Col. 1
Fitters					
Tool room crafts					
Turners					
Pattern makers					
Coppersmiths					
Tinsmiths					
Blacksmiths					
Millwrights					
Moulders					
Sht. met. & pan. beaters					
Founders					
Platers					
Coremakers					
Toolmakers (all types)					
Machine tool setters					
Die setters & sinkers					
Press tool setters					
Carpenters & joiners					
Bricklayers					
Electricians & wiremen					
Electrical testers					
Armature winders					
Coilwinders					
Inst. makers & mech.					
Anglesmiths					
Pipefitters					
Jig borers					
Template makers					

D *The way in which the Craft Apprentices on your firm receive their theoretical and practical training*

Please fill in the number of apprentices in each of the Crafts listed in Column 1 receiving theoretical and practical training in the ways detailed in Columns 2–8 *at the time of filling in the questionnaire.* (In many instances an individual apprentice will be receiving training under a number of headings. In such cases please include him in the total under each of the headings which apply)

If you recruit apprentices to crafts in addition to those shown in Column 1, please add these crafts to the bottom of Column 1 and fill in the relevant details

1 ENGINEERING CRAFTS	2 No. of craft apprentices receiving on the job training (i.e. where boy is apprenticed to a skilled worker from whom he picks up the craft whilst working on production)	3 No. of craft apprentices receiving workshop practice on the firm (i.e. practical training under a skilled supervisor on machines or job used principally for training)	4 No. of craft apprentices receiving workshop practice at part-time day release classes	5 No. of craft apprentices receiving workshop practice at evening technical classes	6 No. of craft apprentices receiving theoretical instruction at part-time day release classes	7 No. of craft apprentices receiving theoretical instruction during working hours (other than part-time day release)	8 No. of craft apprentices receiving theoretical instruction at evening technical classes
Fitters							
Tool room crafts							
Turners							
Pattern makers							
Coppersmiths							
Tinsmiths							
Blacksmiths							
Millwrights							
Moulders							
Sht. met. & pan. beaters							
Founders							
Platers							
Coremakers							
Toolmakers (all types)							
Machine tool setters							
Die setters & sinkers							
Press tool setters							
Carpenters & joiners							
Bricklayers							
Electricians & wiremen							
Electrical testers							
Armature winders							
Coilwinders							
Inst. makers & mech.							
Anglesmiths							
Pipefitters							
Jig borers							
Template makers							

INDEX

209

Index

Brick and tile industry, 13
Bricklayers, 90, 91, 97, 100, 101
Bricklaying, college records, 166–7
British Association for Commercial Education, 38
British Association for Commercial and Industrial Education, 38
British Employers' Confederation, 20
Brunner, Mond and Co., 144
Budgets, household, survey of, 36
Building industry, 10–15, 17, 35, 47, 48, 55, 82 ff., 143, 153, 183, 185, 189, 200
  apprenticeship in, 86–7, 89
  area and size distribution, 51
  categories of firms, 84–5
  constitution of research sample, 56
  craft requirements in, 90
  day release in, 153–4
  distribution of craftsmen, 84
  diversity of firms, 83–4
  inter-craft transfer, 98–9
  method of entry, 98
  proportion of apprentices, 100
  size of firms, 99–100
  structure, 85–6
Building Apprenticeship and Training Council, 88–9, 97
Building Industry National Joint Apprenticeship Scheme, 93 ff.
Building Industry, National Joint Council for, 88, 92–3
'Bulge', effects of, 191

Call-up, see National Service
Cancellation of apprenticeship, 80
Carpenters, 90, 97, 100, 101
Carpenters and joiners (motor vehicle), 128
Carpentry and joinery, college records, 165–6
Census of Production (1948), 50
Central Youth Employment Executive, 23, 29, 34
centres d'apprentissage, 186

certificat d'aptitude professionnelle, 186
Certificates, of competence and training, 95, 101, 107, 125, 176; in U.S.A. 182
  National (Engineering), 144, 149–50
Change-over, from school to employment, 23
Child labour, 2
City and Guilds Institute, 126, 127, 140, 147–9, 175
Clothing trades, 48, 49
Coach builders, 128
Collective Training Centres (Germany), 187
Commercial schools, 142
Committees, Employment, 5
Composition, hand, college records, 167
Compositors, 108, 114, 116
Compositors' unions, 103–4
Conference on Industry and National Service, 134
Conferences, school, 7
Coremakers, 78
Correctors of the Press, Association of, 118
Cost of Living Index, 36
County Colleges, 21, 26, 31, 41, 71, 144, 150, 202
Courses, of technical institutions, 144–5
  technical, proposed grading, 175–6
  question of suitability, 175
Craftsmen's certificate, National (motor vehicle mechanics), 125, 127
Cultural education, 26

Day release, 31–3, 108, 127, 144, 151 ff.
  withdrawal from, 156
Deed of apprenticeship (building), 94
Demarcation, craft, in printing, 119–20

Index

Founded by KARL MANNHEIM
Late Professor of Education in the University of London

Edited by W. J. H. SPROTT
Professor of Philosophy in the University of Nottingham

The International Library

of

Sociology and Social

Reconstruction

ROUTLEDGE & KEGAN PAUL
BROADWAY HOUSE, CARTER LANE, LONDON, E.C.4

SOCIOLOGY OF EDUCATION

Mission of the University
JOSÉ ORTEGA Y GASSET. Translated and introduced by Howard
Lee Nostrand *Second Impression. 12s. 6d.*

Total Education
A Plea for Synthesis
M. L. JACKS, *Director of the Institute of Education, Oxford*
Fourth Impression. 16s.

The Social Psychology of Education
An Introduction and Guide to its Study
C. M. FLEMING, *Reader in Education, Institute of Education, London*
Eighth Impression. 10s.

Education and Society in Modern Germany
R. H. SAMUEL, *Professor of Germanic Languages, Melbourne*, and
R. HINTON THOMAS, *Lecturer in German, Birmingham* 16s.

The Museum
Its History and Its Tasks in Education
ALMA S. WITTLIN *Illustrated. 28s.*

The Educational Thought and Influence of Matthew Arnold
W. F. CONNELL, *Senior Lecturer in Education, Sydney*. With an Introduction by Sir Fred Clarke 23s.

Comparative Education
A Study of Educational Factors and Traditions
NICHOLAS HANS, *Reader in Education, Institute of Education, London*
Fourth Impression. 23s.

New Trends in Education in the 18th Century
NICHOLAS HANS 21s.

From School to University
A Study, with special reference to University Entrance
R. R. DALE, *Lecturer in Education, University College, Swansea* 21s.

Education and Society

An Introduction to the Sociology of Education

A. K. C. OTTAWAY, *Lecturer in Education, Leeds.* With an Introduction by W. O. Lester Smith   *Second Impression.* 18s.

German Youth: Bond or Free

HOWARD BECKER, *Professor of Sociology, University of Wisconsin*
18s.

Parity and Prestige in English Secondary Education

OLIVE BANKS, *Lecturer in Sociology, Liverpool*   25s.

Helvetius

His Life and Place in the History of Educational Thought

IAN CUMMING, *Senior Lecturer in Education, Auckland University College*
25s.

Adolescence

Its Social Psychology: With an Introduction to recent findings from the fields of Anthropology, Physiology, Medicine, Psychometrics and Sociometry

C. M. FLEMING, *Reader in Education, Institute of Education, London*
Fourth Impression. 18s.

Studies in the Social Psychology of Adolescence

J. E. RICHARDSON, J. F. FORRESTER, J. K. SHUKLA and P. J. HIGGINBOTHAM

Edited by C. M. FLEMING   23s.

From Generation to Generation

Age Groups and Social Structure

S. N. EISENSTADT, *Head of the Department of Sociology, Hebrew University, Jerusalem*   42s.

SOCIOLOGY OF RELIGION

Sociology of Religion

JOACHIM WACH, *Professor of the History of Religions, Chicago*   30s.

The Economic Order and Religion

FRANK KNIGHT, *Professor of Social Science, Chicago,* and
THORNTON W. MERRIAM   18s.

3

SOCIOLOGY OF ART AND LITERATURE

Chekhov and His Russia: A Sociological Study
W. H. BRUFORD, *Schröder Professor of German, Cambridge*   18*s*.

The Sociology of Literary Taste
LEVIN L. SCHÜCKING   *Third Impression.* 9*s*. 6*d*.

Men of Letters and the English Public in the 18th Century, 1660-1744, Dryden, Addison, Pope
ALEXANDRE BELJAME, Edited with an Introduction and Notes by Bonamy Dobrée. Translated by E. O. Lorimer   28*s*.

SOCIOLOGICAL APPROACH TO THE STUDY OF HISTORY

The Aftermath of the Napoleonic Wars
The Concert of Europe—An Experiment
H. G. SCHENK, *Lecturer in Political Economics, Fellow of Exeter College, Oxford*   *Illustrated.* 18*s*.

Military Organization and Society
STANISLAW ANDRZEJEWSKI, *Simon Fellow, Manchester.* Foreword by A. Radcliffe-Brown   21*s*.

Population Theories and the Economic Interpretation
SYDNEY COONTZ, *Assistant Professor in Forest Economics, State University of New York, Syracuse*   *In preparation.*

SOCIOLOGY OF LAW

Sociology of Law
GEORGES GURVITCH, *Professor of Sociology, Sorbonne.* With an Introduction by Roscoe Pound   *Second Impression.* 21*s*.

The Institutions of Private Law and their Social Functions
KARL RENNER. Edited with an Introduction and Notes by O. Kahn-Freund   28*s*.

4

Legal Aid

ROBERT EGERTON. With an Introduction by A. L. Goodhart
Second Impression. 12s. 6d.

Soviet Legal Theory: Its Social Background and Development

RUDOLF SCHLESINGER, *Lecturer in Soviet Social and Economic Institutions, Glasgow* *Second Edition.* 28s.

CRIMINOLOGY

Juvenile Delinquency in an English Middletown

HERMANN MANNHEIM, *Reader in Criminology, London School of Economics* 14s.

Criminal Justice and Social Reconstruction

HERMANN MANNHEIM *Second Impression.* 20s.

Group Problems in Crime and Punishment

HERMANN MANNHEIM 28s.

The Psycho-Analytical Approach to Juvenile Delinquency: Theory, Case Studies, Treatment

KATE FRIEDLANDER, *Late Hon. Psychiatrist, Institute for the Scientific Treatment of Delinquency* *Fourth Impression.* 23s.

The English Prison and Borstal Systems

LIONEL FOX, K.C.B., M.C., *Chairman of the Prison Commission for England and Wales* 32s.

Crime and the Services

JOHN SPENCER, *Director of the Bristol Social Project, Bristol University* 28s.

Delinquent Boys: The Culture of the Gang

ALBERT K. COHEN, *Assistant Professor of Sociology, Indiana* 21s.

THE SOCIAL SERVICES

Social Service and Mental Health

An Essay on Psychiatric Social Workers
M. ASHDOWN and S. C. BROWN 18s.

The Social Services of Modern England

M. PENELOPE HALL, *Lecturer in Social Science, Liverpool*
Third Edition (Revised). 28s.

Lunacy, Law and Conscience, 1744-1845
The Social History of the Care of the Insane
KATHLEEN JONES   21s.

British Social Work in the 19th Century
A. F. YOUNG and E. T. ASHTON, *Department of Social Studies,
Southampton University*   25s.

Social Policies for Old Age
B. E. SHENFIELD, *Lecturer in Social Studies, University of Birmingham*
In preparation

SOCIOLOGY AND POLITICS

Social-Economic Movements
An Historical and Comparative Survey of Socialism, Communism, Co-
operation, Utopianism; and Other Systems of Reform and Reconstruc-
tion
H. W. LAIDLER, *Executive Director, League for Industrial Democracy
Second Impression. Illustrated.* 37s. 6d.

*The Analysis of Political Behaviour: An Empirical
Approach*
HAROLD D. LASSWELL, *Professor of Law, Yale. Third Impression.* 23s.

Dictatorship and Political Police
The Technique of Control by Fear
E. K. BRAMSTEDT   20s.

Nationality in History and Politics
A Psychology and Sociology of National Sentiment and Nationalism
FRIEDRICH HERTZ   *Third Impression.* 30s.

The Logic of Liberty: Reflections and Rejoinders
MICHAEL POLANYI, F.R.S., *Professor of Social Studies, Manchester*
18s.

Power and Society
A Framework for Political Inquiry
HAROLD D. LASSWELL, *Professor of Law, Yale,* and
A. KAPLAN, *Professor of Liberal Studies, Indiana*   25s.

The Political Element in the Development of Economic Theory
GUNNAR MYRDAL, *Professor of Economics, Stockholm. Executive Secretary, United Nations Economic Commission for Europe.* Translated from the German by Paul Streeten   25*s.*

Higher Civil Servants in Britain
From 1870 to the Present Day
R. K. KELSALL, *Senior Research Officer, London School of Economics*   25*s.*

Democracy and Dictatorship: Their Psychology and Patterns of Life
Z. BARBU, *Lecturer in Social Psychology, Glasgow*   28*s.*

How People Vote: A Study of Electoral Behaviour in Greenwich
MARK BENNEY, A. P. GRAY, and R. H. PEAR   25*s.*

Economy and Society
A Study in the Integration of Economic and Social Theory
TALCOTT PARSONS, *Chairman of the Department of Social Relations, Harvard,* and NEIL J. SMELSER   35*s.*

The Functions of Social Conflict
LEWIS COSER   18*s.*

FOREIGN AFFAIRS, THEIR SOCIAL, POLITICAL & ECONOMIC FOUNDATIONS

Patterns of Peacemaking
DAVID THOMSON, *Research Fellow, Sidney Sussex College, Cambridge,* E. MEYER and ASA BRIGGS, *Fellow of Worcester College, Oxford* 25*s.*

French Canada in Transition
EVERETT C. HUGHES, *Professor of Sociology, Chicago*   16*s.*

State and Economics in the Middle East
A Society in Transition
A. BONNÉ, *Professor of Economics. Director, Economic Research Institute, Hebrew University, Jerusalem*   *Second Edition (Revised).* 40*s.*

The Economic Development of the Middle East
An Outline of Planned Reconstruction
A. BONNÉ   *Third Impression. 16s.*

Peasant Renaissance in Yugoslavia, 1900-1950
A Study of the Development of Yugoslav Peasant Society as Affected by Education
RUTH TROUTON   28s.

Transitional Economic Systems
The Polish-Czech Example
DOROTHY W. DOUGLAS   25s.

Political Thought in France from the Revolution to the Fourth Republic
J. P. MAYER   14s.

Central European Democracy and its Background
Economic and Political Group Organization
RUDOLF SCHLESINGER   30s.

ECONOMIC PLANNING

Private Corporations and their Control
A. B. LEVY   *Two Volumes. 70s. the set*

The Shops of Britain
A Study of Retail Distribution
HERMANN LEVY   *Second Impression. 21s.*

SOCIOLOGY OF THE FAMILY AND ALLIED TOPICS

The Family and Democratic Society
J. K. FOLSOM, *Professor of Economics, Vassar College*   35s.

Nation and Family
The Swedish Experiment in Democratic Family and Population Policy
ALVA MYRDAL, *Swedish Ambassador to India*

Second Impression. 28s.

The Deprived and the Privileged
Personality Development in English Society
B. M. SPINLEY, *Educational Psychologist, Sheffield Child Guidance Clinic* 20s.

Prosperity and Parenthood
J. A. BANKS, *Assistant Lecturer in Sociology, Liverpool*   21s.

Family, Socialization and Interaction Process
TALCOTT PARSONS and ROBERT F. BALES, *Lecturer in Sociology,*
Harvard University   30s.

The Home and Social Status
DENNIS CHAPMAN, *Senior Lecturer in Social Science, Liverpool University*
119 *tables, diagrams and plates,* 35s.

Women's Two Roles
Home and Work :
ALVA MYRDAL, and VIOLA KLEIN

25s.

TOWN AND COUNTRY PLANNING.
HUMAN ECOLOGY

The Social Background of a Plan: A Study of Middlesbrough
Edited by RUTH GLASS. With Maps and Plans   42s.

City, Region and Regionalism
A Geographical Contribution to Human Ecology
ROBERT E. DICKINSON. With Maps and Plans
Second Impression. 25s.

The West European City: A Study in Urban Geography
ROBERT E. DICKINSON. With Maps and Plans   42s.

Revolution of Environment
E. A. GUTKIND   *Illustrated.* 32s.

The Journey to Work
Its Significance for Industrial and Community Life
K. LIEPMANN, *Research Fellow in Economics, Bristol.* With a Foreword
by Sir Alexander Carr-Saunders   *Second Impression* 16s.

Stevenage: A Sociological Study of a New Town
HAROLD ORLANS   30s.

The Genesis of Modern British Town Planning
A Study in Economic and Social History of the Nineteenth and Twentieth
Centuries
W. ASHWORTH, *Lecturer in Economic History, London School of Economics*
                                                                    21s.

SOCIOLOGICAL STUDIES OF MODERN COMMUNITIES

Negroes in Britain
A Study of Racial Relations in English Society
K. L. LITTLE, *Reader in Anthropology, Edinburgh*   25s.

Co-operative Living in Palestine
HENRIK F. INFIELD. With a Foreword by General
Sir Arthur Wauchope   *Illustrated.* 12s. 6d.

Co-operative Communities at Work
HENRIK F. INFIELD   18s.

Colour Prejudice in Britain
A Study of West Indian Workers in Liverpool, 1941-1951
ANTHONY H. RICHMOND, *Lecturer in Social Theory, Edinburgh*   18s.

Social Mobility in Britain
Edited by DAVID V. GLASS, *Professor of Sociology, London School of
Economics*   36s.

The Absorption of Immigrants
S. N. EISENSTADT   25s.

Studies in Class Structure
G. D. H. COLE, *Chichele Professor of Social and Political Theory, Oxford*
                                                                    21s.

The Study of Groups
JOSEPHINE KLEIN, *Lecturer in Social Studies, Birmingham*   21s.

SOCIOLOGY OF INDUSTRY

Mobility in the Labour Market
MARGOT JEFFERYS, *Lecturer, London School of Hygiene and Tropical Medicine*   15*s.*

Patterns of Industrial Bureaucracy
ALVIN W. GOULDNER, *Professor of Sociology, Illinois*   21*s.*

Wildcat Strike
A Study of an Unofficial Strike
ALVIN W. GOULDNER   16*s.*

ANTHROPOLOGY & RURAL SOCIOLOGY

The Sociology of Colonies: An Introduction to the Study of Race Contact
RENÉ MAUNIER, *Member of the French Academy of Colonial Sciences.*
Translated from the French by E. O. Lorimer *Two volumes.* 63*s. the set*

A Chinese Village: Taitou, Shantung Province
MARTIN C. YANG   23*s.*

A Japanese Village: Suye Mura
JOHN F. EMBREE, *Associate Professor of Anthropology, California.* With an Introduction by A. R. Radcliffe-Brown   *Illustrated.* 21*s.*

The Golden Wing: A Sociological Study of Chinese Familism
YUEH-HWA LIN, *Professor of Social Anthropology, Yenching.* Introduction by Raymond Firth   18*s.*

Earthbound China: A Study of Rural Economy in Yunnan
HSIAO-TUNG FEI, *Professor of Sociology, National Yunnan,* and CHIH-I CHANG, *Lecturer in Sociology, National Yunnan Illustrated.* 20*s.*

Under the Ancestors' Shadow: Chinese Culture and Personality
FRANCIS L. K. HSU, *Professor of Anthropology, College of Liberal Arts, North Western University*   *Illustrated.* 21*s.*

Transformation Scene: The Changing Culture of a New Guinea Village

H. IAN HOGBIN, *Reader in Anthropology, Sydney*   *Illustrated.* 30s.

Indians of the Andes: Aymaras and Quechuas

HAROLD OSBORNE   *Illustrated.* 25s.

Religion, Science and Human Crises

A Study of China in Transition and Its Implications for the West

FRANCIS L. K. HSU   14s.

The Family Herds

P. H. GULLIVER, *Government Sociologist, Tanganyika*   *Illustrated.* 25s.

Growing Up in an Egyptian Village

HAMED AMMAR, *Lecturer in the Sociology of Education, Heliopolis University, Cairo*   28s.

Indian Village

S. C. DUBE, *Professor of Sociology, Osmania University, Hyderabad*   25s.

The Sociology of an English Village : Gosforth

W. M. WILLIAMS, *Lecturer in Geography, University College, North Staffs.*   25s.

Rural Depopulation in England and Wales

JOHN SAVILLE, *Lecturer in Economic History, University of Hull*
Dartington Hall Studies of Rural Society   *In preparation*

The Negro Family in British Guiana: Family Structure and Social Status in the Villages

RAYMOND SMITH, *Research Fellow, Institute of Social and Economic Research, University College of West Indies*   28s.

The History of a Soviet Collective Farm

FEDOR BELOV   21s.

SOCIOLOGY AND PSYCHOLOGY OF THE PRESENT CRISIS

Diagnosis of Our Time
Wartime Essays of a Sociologist
KARL MANNHEIM   18s.

Farewell to European History or the Conquest of Nihilism
ALFRED WEBER   18s.

The Fear of Freedom
ERICH FROMM   21s.

The Sane Society
ERICH FROMM   25s.

Freedom, Power, and Democratic Planning
KARL MANNHEIM. Edited by Hans Gerth and E. K. Bramstedt 28s.

Essays on Sociology and Social Psychology
KARL MANNHEIM. Edited by Paul Kecskemeti   28s.

Essays on the Sociology of Culture
KARL MANNHEIM. Edited by Ernest Manheim and Paul
Kecskemeti   28s.

SOCIAL PSYCHOLOGY AND PSYCHO-ANALYSIS

Psychology and the Social Pattern
JULIAN BLACKBURN, *Associate Professor of Psychology, McGill University, Canada*   *Fifth Impression.* 14s.

The Framework of Human Behaviour
JULIAN BLACKBURN   *Second Impression.* 15s.

A Handbook of Social Psychology
KIMBALL YOUNG, *Professor of Sociology, North-western University*
                                   Fifth Impression. 30s.

Solitude and Privacy
A Study of Social Isolation, Its Causes and Therapy
PAUL HALMOS, *Lecturer in Social Psychology, Social Studies Dept., South West Essex Technical College*   21s.

14

PHILOSOPHICAL AND SOCIAL FOUNDATIONS OF THOUGHT

Homo Ludens: A Study of the Play Element in Culture
J. HUIZINGA   18s.

The Ideal Foundations of Economic Thought
Three Essays on the Philosophy of Economics
WERNER STARK, *Reader in Economics, Manchester*
Third Impression.   16s.

The History of Economics in its Relation to Social Development
WERNER STARK   *Third Impression.*   12s.

America: Ideal and Reality
The United States of 1776 in Contemporary European Philosophy
WERNER STARK   12s.

The Decline of Liberalism as an Ideology
With Particular Reference to German Politico-Legal Thought
J. H. HALLOWELL   14s.

Society and Nature: A Sociological Inquiry
HANS KELSEN, *Department of Political Science, California*   25s.

Marx: His Time and Ours
R. SCHLESINGER   *Second Impression.*   32s.

The Philosophy of Wilhelm Dilthey
H. A. HODGES, *Professor of Philosophy, Reading*   30s.

Essays on the Sociology of Knowledge
KARL MANNHEIM   28s.

GENERAL SOCIOLOGY

A Handbook of Sociology
W. F. OGBURN, *Professor of Sociology, Chicago,* and
M. F. NIMKOFF, *Professor of Sociology, Bucknell*
Third Edition (Revised).   30s.

Social Organization
ROBERT H. LOWIE, *late Professor of Anthropology, Chicago*   35s.

FOREIGN CLASSICS OF SOCIOLOGY

Wilhelm Dilthey: An Introduction

A comprehensive account of his sociological and philosophical work, with translations of selected passages.

H. A. HODGES   *Second Impression.* 14s.

From Max Weber: Essays in Sociology

Translated, Edited and with an Introduction by H. H. GERTH and C. W. MILLS   *Second Impression.* 28s.

Suicide: A Study in Sociology

EMILE DURKHEIM. Translated by J. A. Spaulding and George Simpson   28s.

Community and Association

FERDINAND TONNIES. Edited and supplemented by Charles P. Loomis   21s.

DOCUMENTARY

Changing Attitudes in Soviet Russia

Documents and Readings. Edited with an Introduction by
RUDOLF SCHLESINGER

Volume 1: *The Family in the U.S.S.R.*   30s.

Volume 2: *The Nationalities Problem and Soviet Administration*   30s.

Psychology in the Soviet Union

BRIAN SIMON, *Lecturer in Education, University College, Leicester*
                          In preparation

Soviet Youth: Some Achievements and Problems

Excerpts from the Soviet Press
Edited and translated by DOROTHEA L. MEEK   *In preparation*

All prices are net

1956   Clarke, Doble & Brendon, Ltd., Oakfield Press, Plymouth

331.115
W717r